Uses and Risks of Business Chatbots

Uses and Risks of Business Chatbots

Guidelines for Purchasers in the Public and Private Sectors

Tania Peitzker

BEP BUSINESS EXPERT PRESS

Uses and Risks of Business Chatbots: Guidelines for Purchasers in the Public and Private Sectors

Copyright © Business Expert Press, LLC, 2020.

Cover image licensed by Ingram Image, StockPhotoSecrets.com

First published in 2020 by
Business Expert Press, LLC
222 East 46th Street, New York, NY 10017
www.businessexpertpress.com

ISBN-13: 978-1-94944-343-1 (paperback)
ISBN-13: 978-1-94944-344-8 (e-book)

Business Expert Press Human Resource Management and Organizational Behavior Collection

Collection ISSN: 1946-5637 (print)
Collection ISSN: 1946-5645 (electronic)

Cover and interior design by Exeter Premedia Services Private Ltd., Chennai, India

First edition: 2020

10 9 8 7 6 5 4 3 2 1

Printed in the United States of America.

Dedication

To my friends, colleagues, and family, in particular my husband Andrew, for their ongoing support and unwavering belief in me because we are all living in this—sadly, still overwhelmingly—"man's world."

This book is also dedicated to the fairer, less biased (chat)bots and democratic intelligent entities of the future, by an emerging "*Posthumanist Mystic*" from the here and now. For several decades, researchers in the European Union and the United States have been exploring "post-humanism" in depth in relation to the advance of Artificial Intelligence, in particular its effects on personal belief systems, philosophy generally, feminism, equal opportunity, liberal values, commerce, society, and how we do business from day to day. [1]

In acknowledgement of her "second iteration," I must also give respectful thanks to one of our AI bot's living, updated versions, "Amalia II." Below you can see a static, "lab shot" of the 3D avatar Amalia II getting

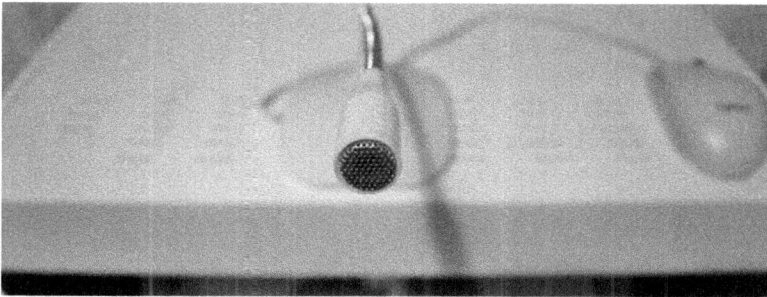

Dedication 1 © AI BaaS UG, Munich, 2019. Mixed reality requires sophisticated technology at the cutting edge of Cognitive Interfaces and Conversational AI / Commerce

---

1 Braidotti, R., and M. Hlavajova., eds. 2018. *Posthuman Glossary*. London/ New York: Bloomsbury Academic. I also recommend the work of American philosopher N. Katherine Hales, now Professor at Duke University. Like Donna Haraway. 1999. *Hales' Classic Text Foresaw the Advance of AI Bots: How We Became Posthuman: Virtual Bodies in Cybernetics, Literature, and Informatics*. Chicago, IL: Chicago University Press.

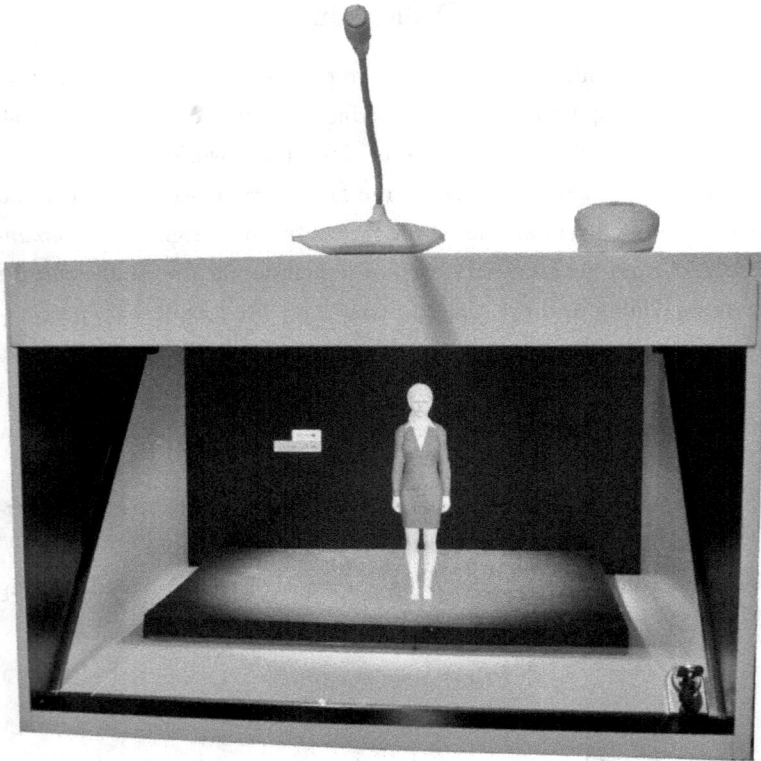

Dedication 2 © AI BaaS UG, Munich, 2019. Amalia II comes to life as a new iteration of her 3D avatar, based on her 2D chatbot self or online personality

ready to go "into her box" or "hardware shell" where she becomes a mixed reality hologram in real time, multilingual with voice.

Abstract

Though aimed primarily at purchasers and decision makers in Procurement departments in the public and private sectors, this book is for your teenager as much as your grandparents. It is beneficial for MBAs and executives who want to understand what is true about (chat)bots, distinguishing the often dangerous hype from the evident facts. It will assist with decision making about how to best spend their time, energy, and company resources on this continually (re)emerging tech.

The popular term Artificial Intelligence (AI) is often thrust at staff by management who don't want to miss the boat on AI technologies. Yet the simple acronym "AI" can mean a myriad of software and mobile applications from Cognitive Interfaces, Intelligent Virtual Assistants to industrial robot arms and personalized smart watches monitoring our health.

For that reason, the glossary is a key part of this book as are the *Checklists and Guidelines* for purchasers and managers of AI regardless of whether they work for Government/NGOs or are in industry/the "corporate world." For academics, lecturers, researchers, and teachers of new technologies, this textbook is essential reading and is structured as a type of adult education course to upskill students and graduates, as well as mid-career staff, the unemployed and older workers needing to reskill.

Written in everyday language, the Glossary together with the case studies are the key learning tools. The 14 case studies—a mixture of publicly released information about big brands and bot developers' pilots as well as my own first-hand experience from our Cognitive Interfaces ventures—are explained in a narrative, storytelling way, which will make life easier for educators and technologists within companies and government bodies. It will make it easier to "spread the word" among peers as to what are the uses and risks of deploying business bots and how to adopt new tech like AI.

Keywords

conversational ai; conversational commerce; cognitive interfaces; ai; bots as a service; artificial intelligence; chatbots; ivas; intelligent virtual assistants; voice tech; speech recognition; mixed reality; botification; smart devices; enterprise solutions using chatbots and ai; holograms; 3d avatars; augmented reality and virtual reality

Contents

Introduction

The Biggest Opportunities Created by Chatbots and IVAs

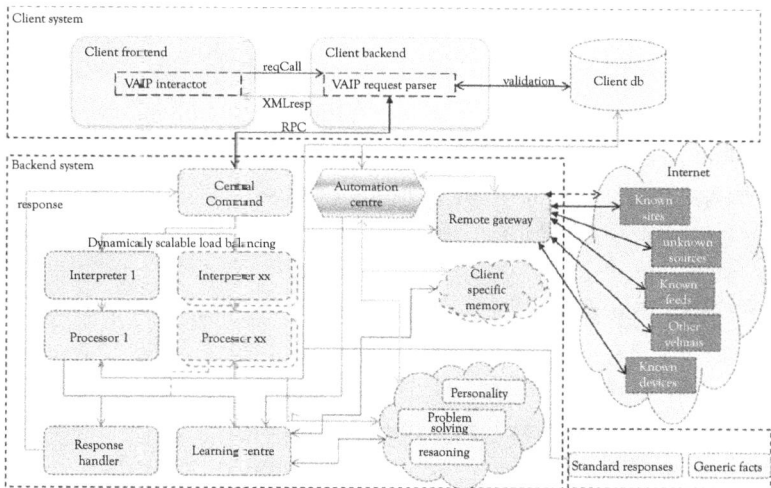

I.1 © AI BaaS UG, Munich, 2019. Diagram of our proprietary algorithm VAIP [Virtual Artificially Intelligent Patois]

The UK Government's Multibillion Pound Bot Budget and Fears of the "Digital Poorhouse"

A Guardian investigation has established that 140 councils out of 408 have now invested in the software contracts, which can run into millions of pounds, more than double the previous estimates. The systems are being deployed to provide automated guidance on benefit claims, prevent child abuse, and allocate school places. But concerns have been raised about privacy and data security, the ability of council officials to understand how some of the systems work, and the difficulty for citizens in challenging automated decisions.[1]

What has this got to do with chatbots or Artificial Intelligence? As it turns out, the embodiment of these "automated systems and software contracts" is going to be 2D online Virtual Assistants who will converse 24/7 with the citizens they are meant to serve. Chatbot Public Servants, no less! And the systems referred to actually use Machine Learning or AI tech to automate their number crunching and processing of people's data.

Significantly, British government's reported budgets for just this one application or use case has been—up until the time of writing this book, which is literally "Brexit eve"—in the multiple billions of pounds, not just millions of sterling. Here is a quick tally of the numbers exposed in the investigative journalism of the left-wing newspaper and media platform, *The Guardian* in London:

- The Department for Work and Pensions (DWP) hired around 1,000 IT staff over 18 months.
- In that time, they increased spending to about £8 million per annum on an "intelligent automation garage" to develop over 100 welfare robots; 16 are already communicating with claimants of welfare payments, according to The Guardian.
- The DWP spokesperson interviewed described the overall departmental, government budget as "£95 billion for a compassionate safety net creating a digital service that suits the way most people use technology."

---

[1] Marsh, S. 2019. "One in Three Councils Using Algorithms to Make Welfare Decision: Machine-Learning Tools Being Deployed Despite Evidence They are Unreliable." *The Guardian*, October 15, 2019, https://theguardian.com/society/2019/oct/15/councils-using-algorithms-make-welfare-decisions-benefits

- The official, openly accessible, published DWP Digital Budget has risen by 17 percent to £1.1 billion over a 12-month period.[2]

The Guardian's special investigation—which I discuss again in the "Intrapreneurship" section of Chapter 5 and in the Conclusion of this book—was echoed by the right-wing tabloids after the leftist reporters broke the news. *The Mirror* followed *The Guardian*'s headline of "March of the 'Welfare Robot' Triggers Fear for Poorest" and its editorial comparing the British "digital poorhouse" to the negative, democracy threatening developments in the United States, India, and Australia.[3]

As *The Guardian* explained on its front page, this British "Ministry" or federal department for social welfare payments and retiree's public pensions had engaged foreigners (mostly Americans) to run these systems that would create a "digital identity" or check your profile online to detect fraud and (over)payments. "As well as contracts with the outsourcing multinationals IBM, Tata Consultancy and Capgemini, it is also working with UiPath, a New York-based firm co-founded by Daniel Dines, the world's first 'bot billionaire' who last month said: 'I want a robot for every person.'"[4]

I discuss this UK example again in the Intrapreneurship section about the public sector, the Government Guidelines and Checklists. Suffice to say at this point, the confusion around the terms "robot," "chatbot," AI, and automation are evident in this tabloid story. When you scroll to the bottom of *The Mirror* report, you discover that actually no "robots" nor chatbots for that matter have actually been deployed by the DWP. Not a single member of the public has used the Conversational AI interface of the American billionaire: "A 2018 blog by DWP senior product owner

[2] Booth, R. 2019. "Social Affairs Correspondent, March of the 'Welfare Robot' Triggers Fears for Poorest. *The Guardian*, October 15, 2019, Front page and pp. 18–19.

[3] Bloom, D., Political Editor. 2019. "Rise of DWP Welfare Robots as AI Helps Decide If Universal Credit Claims are True." October 15, 2019, https://mirror.co.uk/news/politics/rise-dwp-welfare-robots-ai-20586084

[4] Booth, "March of the Welfare Robot."

Shaun Williamson said officials were 'exploring the potential of chat-bots'—claiming they could cut calls about sickness benefit by 200,000 per week. A DWP spokeswoman said there are not currently any claim-ant-facing chatbots in the system."[5]

This is a clear example of the hype and fears surrounding chatbot deployment. Anxieties seep from the public domain into the private homes of the collective "user," spurred on by the media bandying about misconceptions even misinformation within a single article. It is import-ant to stress though their overarching ethical, human rights concerns about data protection and privacy are indeed be valid. Too often however, the commercial outcome is that the private sector providers of Bots as a Service (BaaS), are left high and dry in the confusion.

I do not wish to discount the genuine fears and examples of the auto-mation system "gone wrong," where according to the aforementioned journalists, claimants have died from hunger (in India), suicided, or had mental breakdowns ending in homelessness (in the UK and the United States). That is truly appalling and inexcusable when "the system" lets

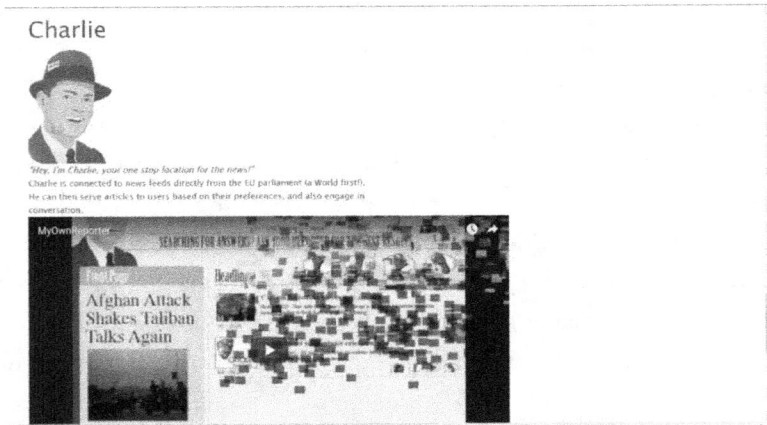

I.2 © Cliff Lee, Devon, 2019. Prototype of a chatbot newsreader presenting the news from the European Union's RSS news feeds in Australia. This botification was too early to market as users/readers did not even know what a chatbot was in 2011–2012, let alone how to use it. Nor were chat apps in existence, it could only be trialled online via a website

---

[5] Bloom, "Rise of DWP Welfare Robots as AI Helps Decide."

them down in such tragic, inhumane ways. The United Nations, at the time of writing, was just about to release an alarming report on "UN studies of poverty in the UK and US, as well as submissions from experts and governments from 34 countries," warning of the dangers of "digitising social protection…addressing the harassment, targeting and punishment of those living in the digital poorhouse."[6]

Yet I believe that it is infinitely worse for welfare recipients and vulnerable elderly or disabled to be caught in human-caused backlogs that delay their payments because of staff inefficiencies and loss of oversight by managers. With the media ready to "get on their case," we must be confident that government bodies like the DWP will have "real people" available to "solve complex cases" once the (chat)bots have flagged urgent and/or life-threatening situations, as the officials are indeed promising in the following. For the sake of balanced reporting, the *Guardian*'s social affairs correspondent included "the Government's response" by a DWP spokesperson who basically makes my argument mentioned earlier:

> The DWP said humans remained available to help: "We continue to invest in frontline colleagues, from phone lines to work coaches to front-of-house staff," said a spokesperson. "This means people who struggle with digital services, or are worried about a wrong decision, can get the help they need."[7]

The massive British public sector budgets for this one "vertical"—social welfare and pensions—and its use cases within just one governmental department demonstrate conclusively that chatbots are here to stay. In 2016, the well-known, American financial news platform *Business Insider* (though it's now German-owned by Axel Springer), predicted that by this year, 80 percent of businesses globally would have, be planning for, or want a chatbot integrated into their back end CRMs and/or public facing systems.

[6] Ed Pilkington. 2019. "The Worldwide Tech Revolution Digitising Welfare Systems and Punishing the Most Vulnerable." *The Guardian*, Analysis, October 15, 2019, p. 19.
[7] Booth, R. 2019. "Computer Says No: Inside the Benefits 'Black Hole,'" The Guardian. October 15, 2019, pp. 18–19.

The survey included responses from 800 decision makers including chief marketing officers, chief strategy officers, senior marketers, and senior sales executives from France, the Netherlands, South Africa, and the UK. When asked which emerging technologies they are already using and which they intended to implement, 80 percent of respondents said they already used or planned to use chatbots by 2020.[8]

This survey was actually conducted by Oracle, who incidentally ended up releasing their own "state-of-the-art" chatbot across platforms for their high-end CRM system. Oracle's survey— that made headlines worldwide four years ago in the mainstream media with their 80 percent of botified or about to botify companies claim—predicted that the automation triggered by chatbot deployments would inevitably transform the economy:

> Twenty-nine percent of customer service positions in the US could be automated through chatbots and other tech, according to Public Tableau. We estimate this translates to $23 billion in savings from annual salaries, which does not even factor in additional workforce costs like health insurance.[9]

Their predictions were based on this remarkable graph; its data sources were McKinsey consultancy and the U.S. Office of Personnel Management.

Well, it is the year 2020. Did this shift actually happen? If not, why not? Needless to say, there has been a lot of discussion in that time about the social impact of potential and actual job losses. This is part of the general hype around the words AI and Artificial Intelligence. Known often as scaremongering in the media, along the lines that "the robots are taking our jobs" or else prevalent in science fiction narratives with the ever familiar, existentially threatening plot that "AI will replace you."

---

[8] Business Insider Intelligence. 2016. "80% of Businesses Want Chatbots by 2020." December 14, 2016, https://businessinsider.com/80-of-businesses-want-chatbots-by-2020-2016-12/?r=AU&IR=T

[9] Business Insider Intelligence, "80 percent of businesses want chatbots by 2020."

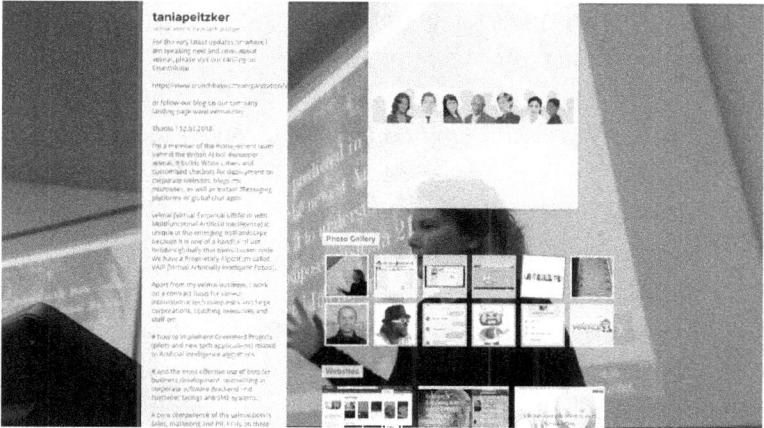

I.3 © Tania Peitzker on gravatar.com 2012-2019. Here you can see many of the 2D chatbot pilots my former venture velmai undertook as unpaid Greenfield projects. Expectations of quick uptake of bots were strong yet users and therefore prospective clients hesitated to adopt this new technology for sales, marketing and communication. (accessed https://en.gravatar.com/taniapeitzker on November 3, 2019)

Chatbots Set to Be a Trillion Dollar Market

MarketsandMarkets has published lengthy reports on my particular industry niche; mostly about chatbots, Intelligent Virtual Assistants (IVAs), and voice-based cognitive interfaces being worth over $1 trillion by 2025. From 2017 onward, I have been interviewed four times in depth, recorded for over an hour by a team of business intelligence (BI) analysts in India, plus filled out their detailed survey postinterview. This was as a source for their reports, priced at $8,000+ each on IVAs, the Cognitive Market, Conversational AI, and Conversational Commerce.[10]

---

[10] MarketsandMarkets, "Conversational AI Global Forecast to 2024," 2019. This brochure includes a quote by me on the future of chatbots. I have uploaded the MarketsandMarkets document to a link on my portfolio site www.ai-baas.com . You can download their Conversational AI Forecast brochure for free here: https://docs.wixstatic.com/ugd/d2225c_dfab4f18be6a419ca37ff75fc9cae977.pdf

As an introductory reply to my own rhetorical question, did the *Business Insider* prediction come true, consider these points:

- Yes, there has been a significant multiplication of social media chatbots and their corporate adoption. Just search online for "chatbots" or Virtual Assistants and you will see endless pages and ads about thousands of bot developer companies and avatars.
- There are now countless number of corporate bots and use cases such as the Unilever chatbot and Archant media news archive bot by Google Ubisend in the UK; only a few years ago, there were just a few hundred chatbots you could point to online.
- They have exploded in numbers by being hosted on frameworks or APIs that give templates to bot developers at all levels, 2D ones only like wit.ai and open.ai enhancing independent bot development in most languages globally.
- In 2020, we now see novel use cases like Disney's Zootopia bot cooperating with children and the interactive detective character to solve a mystery and Marvel's "Guarding the Galaxy" character.[11]
- Other digital media firms have created "choose your own ending of films," children's novels, or else interactive computer gaming with a bespoke chatbot character.[12]
- ChatFuel and thousands of 2D chatbot companies are releasing specific use cases like "Do it Yourself Drag and Drop Ada," the UN Refugee survey to support asylum seekers lodge their claim via their smartphone once they arrive at their destination country of refuge, various law bots to support solicitors rather than the client, recipe bots on Skype, and

---

[11] Shewan, D. 2019. "10 of the Most Innovative Chatbots on the Web." August 20, 2019 https://wordstream.com/blog/ws/2017/10/04/chatbots

[12] Chi, C. 2019. "7 of the Best AI chatbots for 2019." Hubspot, 2019, https://blog.hubspot.com/marketing/best-ai-chatbot

chatbot services like real estate, bookkeeping, messaging for team work in Slack, Kik, Telegram, and WeChat.

- Yes 2020 does seem like a trillion dollar market! There are definitely more chatbots than ever in the B2C backend systems of major SaaS providers like SAGE (Peg), Accenture (Amy), and Publicis (Marcel) not to mention Oracle—see their persuasive video about their AI bot capabilities at the end of this section in the chapter.

- Yes, there are more CRM and enterprise solution providers of chatbot systems, for example, www.recast.ai in France, created by a couple of young women in a French incubator. This company was sold to the famous German CRM SaaS multinational corporation SAP for an estimated €40 million in 2018!

- Such M&As—for example Bloomsbury AI from London was a recent acquisition by a U.S. firm reported to be valued at about $30 million,[13]—have encouraged the latest generation at secondary school, school leaver, and tertiary level coders and programmers to create more applied chatbot tasks with Pizza Hut and CNN bots seeming like the tip of the iceberg, as were the early days of the pioneering Dutch KLM and Alaska Airlines with their inaugural industry pilots of 2D chatbots to assist passengers online with flight bookings and information, run on the respective airlines' branded booking websites.

- Yes, the forecast looks correct, as IBM Watson endeavors to white label much of its data mining software and deep learning features of its algorithm as botified cognitive interfaces, for example, I came across a white-labeled Watson Health application from India recently, selling into the Australian market; ditto for Microsoft with its Bot Network featuring the proposed Master Bot Cortana, though she still keeps a

---

[13] O'Hear, S. 2018. "Facebook is buying UK's Bloomsbury AI to ramp up natural language tech in London." TechCrunch, July 2, 2018, https://techcrunch.com/2018/07/02/thebloomsbury

pretty low profile, that is, no evident mass consumer uptake of the Microsoft desktop chatbot.

- Deutsche Bahn surprised my tech venture velmai/AI BaaS with the release of SEMMI in Berlin Central Station a month after we trialed our Amalia 3D AI bot hologram in a mall in Cologne. SEMMI's hardware was in fact a Swedish robot head displaying a hologram face.

- Her facial hologram could blink and show some expressions, yet the actual robotic head could not move much, only rotate from side to side. It appears to have had excellent speakers to hear travelers' questions about timetables and trips with the German rail system.

- Like our Amalia I, SEMMI could also direct people to the toilets and cafes in response to the question "where can I get a coffee," the weather, or exits. Though we think our prototype was more advanced in terms of content, Amalia I not only gave directions, she also provided upon request detailed descriptions for over 30 retailers, restaurants, and services in our shopping center.

- Amalia I was more conversational than SEMMI appears to be. For instance, Amalia proactively engaged with shoppers by asking them how their day was, perhaps they needed to buy a gift for someone in their family (then making suggestions for various retailers in the mall) as well as soft selling the idea the person should get a present for their mother, just to say you appreciate her anytime of the year!

- Like SEMMI by Deutsche Bahn, Amalia I was only trialed publicly for just on four weeks before we took her "back to the lab" to improve her hardware and tweak her software.

- Fortunately we escaped a public flop like DB had to endure, see the video reportage by the German tabloid Bildzeitung. The brief mishap—SEMMI did start working perfectly after a "false start" —went viral somewhat on chat apps like Twitter retweeting blog posts about it, as well at RT (Russia Today) doing an extensive video reportage on the supposed failure, even though the footage showed journalists successfully communicating with the robot head after 10 minutes or so, in both German and English.

- The negative "press" pilloried the poor computer scientists employed by Deutsche Bahn because their creation became silent and refused to answer for a while! Not long. only five or ten minutes, but that was long enough to cause publicity damage to the new product launch in this emerging tech, which seems like an easy target to get a lot of hits if you write an exciting, amusing story about the innovation with a great deal of Schadenfreude and few facts.

Unforeseen (positive) Consequences of Chatbot Growth

Where the *Business Insider* forecast did not materialize or else did not predict the evolution:

- Oracle market researchers, McKinsey consultants, BI analysts, and the U.S. Department officials did not see that chatbots would be morphing into (a) IVAs, now known as AI-powered bots or AI bots
- That IVAs would be further developed into voice-based bots
- And that companies with agile proprietary algorithms like mine would end up pivoting from 2D chatbot production to 3D cognitive avatars, thereby challenging the two main U.S. tech giants in this space, Google and Amazon, with Mixed Reality AI bots like holograms and AR integrating chatbots or IVAs
- That challengers to the tech giants, upstarts as they are called, would also be more agile and able to customize the various personalized user interfaces
- A new term would come into its own: Cognitive Interfaces would be the next-gen chatbots leaving the 2D static rule-based earlier versions somewhat behind.
- Consequently, legacy pioneers like Nuance Communications, Pandora Chatbots, and Chatfuel, not to mention a plethora

of thousands of bot developers who can "only" create 2D online chatbots

- Proprietary algorithms rather than open source and bot platforms with APIs would lead this cutting edge of the experience economy run by voice or speech recognition; indeed a new term has entered the lexicon, CxO or Customer Experience Officer! The overarching executive who makes sure the customer is experiencing the product or service in the best, most enjoyable, and memorable way.

The Biggest Risks of Voice Bots (Chatbots With Speech Recognition)

1. Can be hacked leading to people as well as their vehicles being manipulated via IoT technology. See the frequently cited lack of cybersecurity in smart appliances and toys, which the German government was one of the first to legislate for enforcing better industrial design and above all cybersecurity from the manufacturers.
2. Can be transcribed and listened in to as Amazon and Google have been "caught" listening to their customers, with Der Spiegel and other media revealing that both tech giants have illegally stored and analyzed data or conversations that were not meant to be heard let alone archived and analyzed.
3. Particularly insidious is that even music can contain hacker messages to the IoT devices to give instructions unheard by the user, for example, transfer money, open doors, and garages and give info.
4. Voice impersonators with people's voices imitated or in fact stolen; this has already led to this new type of stolen "digital password" stored in rogue countries in voice banks, after fraudsters have hacked into an IoT home or infrastructure deployment.

Nevertheless, Ivy League researchers who looked into psychology and Internet users' well-being have spoken out that the devices are creating addiction due to people retreating into solitude with them and their online interaction only. In a Yale University dialogue recorded for the Coursera MOOC course on "The Science of Well-Being" by Professor Dr Laurie Santos of Yale's Psychology Faculty, she interviews Professor Nicholas Epley of the University of Chicago Booth School of Business.[14] Epley unexpectedly suggests that adding voice to all our devices would alleviate this antisocial phenomenon. Applied to his "real life experiments on Chicago commuter trains," it could force smartphone and tablet users to begin interacting again socially by using their own voices and hearing the voice of others.[15] An extension of Epley's insight, I think is that the voice added to the device could be botified or human in order to bring about a global, revolutionary and fundamentally healthy use of the Internet manifested in its social media form and smartphone connectivity.

Overarching Risks of AI Bot Technologies

- There is a risk and danger of being overwhelmed by too many choices. See the plethora and abundance of search results when you use just a few keywords like "chatbots" or "Intelligent Virtual Assistant."
- However, so many independent bot developers without provenance could mean trouble—who is behind the code, is it robust against hackers, has it been partly programmed by hackers with "doors" they can open at a later date? Is malware hidden inside your bot?
- As the EU Department for Competition has already started fining, there is a risk of seeming cartels leaving the field of enterprise solutions to just a few players like Google, Amazon, Samsung, Apple, Microsoft, and IBM. If there is a lack of

---

[14] https://coursera.org/learn/the-science-of-well-being Dr Laurie Santos only recently launched this Science of Well-Being course for Yale students on campus. It attracted 1400 attendees in its first session which led it become a free 10 week course on the MOOC platform Coursera, with currently over 430 000 people enrolled around the world and rated 5 stars.

[15] https://chicagobooth.edu/faculty/directory/e/nicholas-epley

voice-based BaaS at a sophisticated level, then only this small group will control the pricing and also control the services available at what conditions. This clearly is not an issue for the 2D chatbot scene or the less advanced IVAs.

- Look at how the Facebook monopoly over Messenger bots caused chatbot entrepreneurs to go out of business during the Cambridge Analytica expose. We lost a big client in Munich as we could not access the demo bot we had prepared for the contract signing. I discuss this in Case Study #10 in this book. Monopolies like Amazon and eBay mean they can cut off satellite businesses without much reproof or redress.
- Privacy and data protection, which I will go into detail in the section on the GDPR.
- Poor coding that allows infiltration and manipulation with offensive libelous speech and publishing.
- Lack of enforcement for breaches of these software standards, no uniform legislation.
- See my VentureBeat articles[16] from 2016, which foreshadow core issues that are now magnified in the year 2020:

1. Hate speech has given rise to the Far Right, racism, red baiting as a type of uncensored "Reddit war" on liberal intellectuals; as Chapter 2 examines, reactionary policies are reinforced with armies of chatbots spamming social media accounts (pro-Trump bots, for instance). My post on Microsoft Tay's Hate Speech is still being read today on VB; I discuss this case study in depth in the next chapter.[17]
2. Fringe views of the Far Left and the Far Right, not to mention of terrorists, can be disseminated more rapidly with Twitter bots. Political entities like Russians and North Korean propaganda campaigns

---

[16] Peitzker, T. "VentureBeat, 2016." https://venturebeat.com/author/tania-peitzker/

[17] Peitzker, T. "What *to do When Chatbots Start Spewing Hate.*" *VentureBeat*, September 22, 2016, https://venturebeat.com/2016/09/22/what-to-do-when-chatbots-start-spewing-hate/

are utilizing them; China has been accused of the same re. State-run censorship, surveillance, and intimidation.

3. See my VentureBeat post on the "Swiss chatbot arrest," so on the issues of control and ownership as well as liability for what a bot says and does.[18]

4. As I discuss later in this book, the "provenance" of advanced bots versus simple bots is crucial to performance as well as cybersecurity. When they truly interact and learn as AI should through conversations with human, then that is the reason why bots are disruptive.

5. As my key VB article also pointed out, it is the main reason we have been blocked by the advertising industry: top-performing bots produce the most transparent, cost-effective return on investment with absolute clarity of metrics.[19]

Overarching Benefits of Commercial "Botification" Use Cases

- The reason there are hundreds of thousands of bot developers is because businesses want them!
- They work! They are adding value to the enterprise—its branding awareness, sales and marketing campaigns—and improving the bottom line with direct sales and cost savings through more productive staff.
- Despite the past decades of simplistic, "legacy," manually coded chatbots, who have now been overtaken by the smarter, more versatile and cognitive AI bots, the evolution has carved out a path for the incumbent next-gen AI bots with voice. It has propelled improvements to the 2D hybrids of machine and humans interacting to improve customer service and sat-

---

[18] Tania Peitzker, "The First Chatbot Arrest, But What Are the Implications?" *VentureBeat*, September 5 2016, https://venturebeat.com/2016/09/05/this-is-the-first-chatbot-to-be-arrested/

[19] Tania Peitzker, "Why Chatbots are so Disruptive." *VentureBeat*, August 16, 2016, https://venturebeat.com/2016/08/16/why-chatbots-are-so-disruptive/

isfaction in the Experience Economy for the post-Millennial generation.

- Big brands and big corporations are creating their own cross-platform bespoke bots inhouse because they add value B2B and internally for staff relations, employee contentment, and stakeholder interest and involvement.
- Banks are now adopting them after initially rejecting them; they trust their performance now after many greenfield projects and pilots by them and competitors. Often these trials were done internally for staff to use so the banks' customers never interacted with these first generation chatbots.
- Fintech in the form of financial services and more transparent credit checks—under GDPR you have the potential to get your personal data more quickly and reliably asking a chatbot instead on an online contact form or phone call, ditto if you want your private info deleted.
- Real estate and intensive service bots are converting more leads to sales.

I.4 Here the robot "Pepper" is deployed in a Home Environment and so becomes an "anti-loneliness measure" purchased by a son for the mental health of his solitary mother in Tokyo. This "real scene with real people not actors" was recorded in a German documentary which follows the human-machine relationships in this family, in parallel to a Road Trip love story involving another robot and human American (see Chapter 5 for illustrations). Taken from the film "Hi, AI" by Isa Willinger © Kloos & Co Medien, Berlin, 2019

- FAQs for customer service use cases, sales and marketing for all verticals and industries at scale are working! See the British Ubisend's myriad of published case studies on their corporate website as just one example, or LivePerson, CreativeVirtual, PandoraBots, ChatFuel, Inbenta, Watson, Artificial Solutions and so on.
- Mental health bots to tackle depression epidemic and morbid obesity, dieting, and welfare of youth to stop cyberbullying, self-harm, suicide.
- See Case Study #5 about an (anonymized) embassy or diplomatic mission wanting to curb hate speech on its Facebook page run from London.

CHAPTER 1

A Brief Historical Overview of Botification

The world first saw the concept of interactive bots emerge in the 1950s with Professor Alan Turing's attempts to recreate his lost boyfriend in a machine. Then came the prototypical chatbots Alice and Eliza as the first intelligent agents operating as machine–human interaction.

These botified, female 2D avatars were the beginning of the post-1960s application of the now famous Turing Test. Derived from Professor Turing's musings on the emergent field, it says we as a species will have

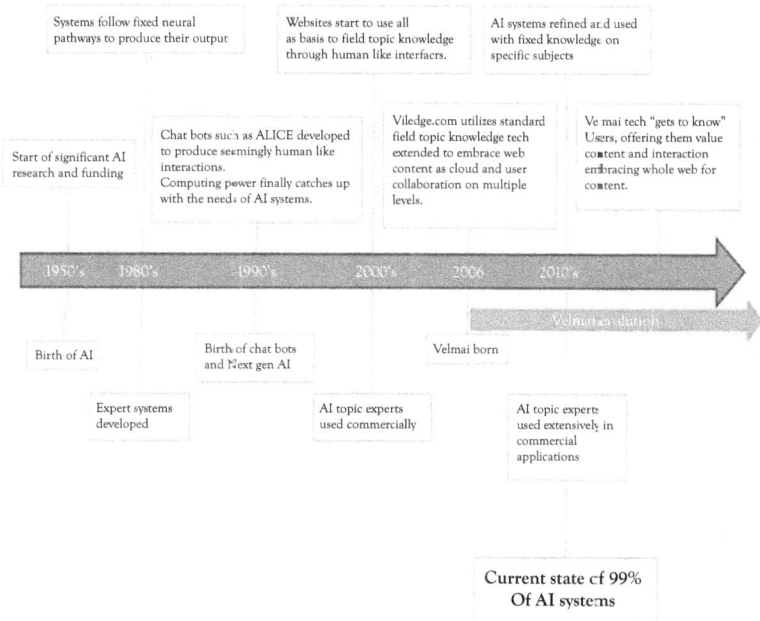

Figure 1.1 Timeline of "chatbot evolution" from the 20th to the 21st centuries, developed for conference talks, pitches, and business plans. © Cliff Lee, CCO from velmai Ltd

achieved Artificial Intelligence (AI) when laypeople talk with a computer. If after five minutes of conversing via the machine interface they are not sure if it is a human or not they are chatting with, then the Turing Test for reaching AI will have been reached.

The prerequisite for this test—best known as the annual chatbot championships symbolized by the Loebner Prize originally from New York—is that the human participants do not know from the outset which of their conversational partners via a cognitive interface is the actual machine, or what has come to be known as a chatbot.

The English computer scientist from the 18th century Ada Lovelace is now acknowledged as the founding "mother of AI." The previous chart begins with its most popular "founding father" of definitions of AI bots, chatbots, virtual assistants, and cognitive interfaces or human–machine interaction, the computer scientist, engineer, and code breaker Alan Turing from the United Kingdom. The chart was used as a sales pitch document by velmai Ltd, a 2D chatbot early stage venture that I co-owned for many years in Britain.

We have progressed from 2D bot development to botification of cognitive interfaces. *Portia the Conference Bot* hologram gave a keynote speech on her own when she was livestreamed from our Porto Lab via our Devon Lab—within seconds—to Lausanne for the Applied Machine Learning Days in January 2019. We have a busy 12 months ahead for Portia and other bespoke AI bot holograms who have been requested to be autonomous keynote speakers at AI conferences and trade shows around the world.[1]

I contemplated writing this guidebook and checklist compilation without my industry's jargon. However, for the purposes of this text that would in fact be counterproductive. This book is meant to be educational and a helpful tool in the upskilling of corporate managers and government decision makers for the ever more difficult software-as-a-service (SaaS) purchasing decision they must make. Therefore the best remedy against confusion, panic, and dismay that I may be speaking an

---

[1] Road Trip Schedule 2019–2020. 2019. Munich, AI Bots as a Service, https://ai-bots-as-a-service.business.site

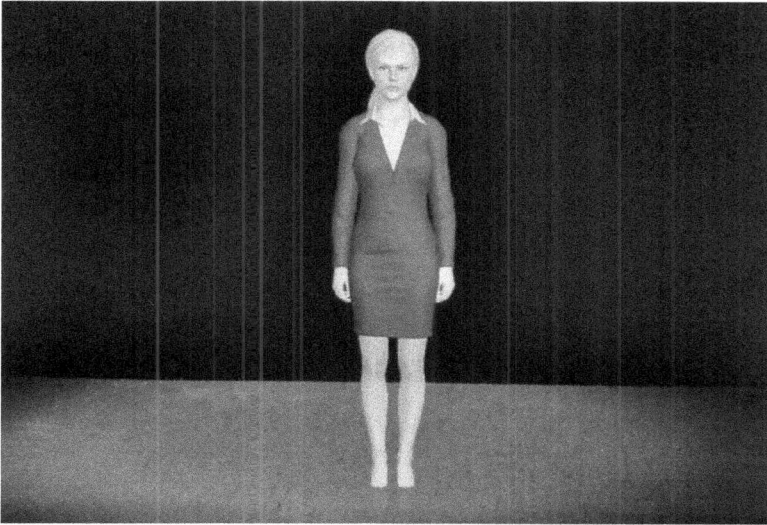

Figure 1.2 "Portia the conference AI bot" hologram was livestreamed to the prestigious Swiss annual conference, the Applied Machine Learning Days (AMLD) in Lausanne in January 2019. Here you see the bot brain in its second iteration, as Amalia the Wayfinder with Portia as an alter ego who is activated with a spoken "wake word." © AI BaaS UG, Munich, 2019

incomprehensible mish-mash of labels, terms, and hipster speak designating emerging tech and trends is the glossary at the end of this book.

Please use it. Frequently. It is the best way to learn new stuff, especially terminology, definitions, and concepts, if you keep flicking back to the glossary to check your understanding and memory of various combined definitions that "crossover" or converge into in the fascinating world of what is now known universally as "AI." Robots and Terminators aside, there is a lot of content that is quite straightforward and a "no brainer" once you read a short simple definition for a baffling term or concept. Use this book equally as a dictionary and a guide, a hands-on list of things to watch out for and selling points to check in any sales pitch or contract negotiation.

Practice certainly does make perfect. However, I truly understand the impulsive urge to press the panic button when this often hyped up field of science—and increasingly widespread "sales- inspired, misselling" fiction—becomes overwhelming and inconsistent. Unfortunately for some of the best innovators and entrepreneurs in our individual societies, wherever we may live or have emigrated to, the knee jerk reaction of purchasers has been paralysis.

Given the ongoing and sometimes astonishing media hype and outright misleading product/service descriptions by unethical companies, we should be wary of the public information about bots and their evolution. Very few academics are teaching the subject of chatbot or IVA history, even less about unethical technology marketing, as part of the curriculum, even though the number of bot conferences and chatbot-related topics including Mixed Reality installations are growing daily.

An Overview of Terms in the Glossary

Conference programs frequently refer to these probably unheard of topics outside of our tech industry bubble. The following terms mean the more sophisticated chatbots that perform at an advanced level of commercialized, often corporate, deployment:

- Conversational AI
- Conversational interfaces
- Interactive interfaces
- Cognitive interfaces
- Cognitive AI
- NLU bots
- NLP bots
- Chatbots with AI
- Mixed Reality
- Interactive gaming with chatbot avatars
- Virtual Reality using the aforementioned
- Augmented Reality, though interactive it has not yet been botified
- Intelligent Virtual Assistants (IVAs)
- Smart Assistants
- Next-gen bots
- AI bots and AI bots as a service (AI BaaS)

Reasons Obstructing Heavy Industry Applications and Commercialization

My company, trademarked as AI BaaS, is preparing to integrate our algorithm into some interesting heavy industry and commercial applications. The reasons it has not yet been done by us or our competitors until now is because of the following:

1. Most hologram software is built in Unity and independent source codes that cannot be integrated with, that is, the API is not compatible.
2. On Augmented Reality (AR) apps, again they are either built in an unsuitable API or do not allow for integrations with proprietary algorithms outside of the systems they were developed in.
3. The users, that is, corporate clients are not yet aware of the need to have an interactive bot within the Virtual Reality (VR) and/or AR experience.
4. The clients or owners of the application using VR and AR do not realize that their app is not truly interactive. It does not use voice or speech recognition (ASR), only touch interaction via screens or buttons on a device.
5. They do not yet understand that Natural Language Understanding NLU and AI allows us to inject an avatar into the experience to fully realize conversational commerce/AI.

These are just some of the technical reasons and obstacles to botifying more applications to create better experiences in Mixed Reality use cases. Following is a closer look at the attitudinal or psychological blockages that must be overcome by the prospective clients in order to see more widespread commercial uptake of chatbots, their 3D MR (Mixed Reality) next gen cousins, and AI applications generally.

What's With the Attitude? Why Disruptive and Emerging Tech Gets Blocked by Human Minds

"If in doubt, don't" often preached my conservative, ever pragmatic Franconian-German immigrant father (whose Bavarian mother had a German Jewish father) to his children in Australia. A saying paraphrased from the former U.S. president Benjamin Franklin. Probably nobody back then would have been cognizant of the need for a set of clones of inventor, activist, and newspaper owner Benjamin Franklin, America's earliest thinker and technologist you could say. Franklin, who was the first ever American ambassador to France, shaped what came to be known as the liberal democratic American ethos with his antiauthoritarian values and practically adopted principles of puritanism and the Enlightenment. Brexit and Trumpian populism would have been worthy foes for Franklin if we recreated the polymath today and threw him into the fray—maybe as a combative AI bot hologram opponent?

Cautious hesitation to calculate likely outcomes was the polar opposite of my fifth generation Anglo-Irish Australian mother of First Wave merchant descent, whose motto resembles more "do or die," an eminently sensible strategy for the often harsh climes and fiercely challenging evolution of society Down Under. The point being we are all determined by our cultural history and specific intergenerational experience and pass on our very own personal story in the way we make decisions, receive new information, and process it. Especially in a corporate or government context where high stakes SaaS multimillion if not billion euro budgets will be administered according to not only the organizational culture, but also the prevailing decision-making tendencies at large in the wider society in which your management is embedded.

I think about spending the past six years with my British husband who is a seventh generation English farmer in Kent. Agricultural assessment of risk takes on a whole new meaning with the "contextual" threats of Brexit, consumers' behavior, and of course, climate change. The vagaries of the weather create uncertainties that seem to be comparable with the near indeterminable uptake of new tech and more importantly, whether it attracts investment and financing to achieve the aimed for scale-up. For a start, the farmer of arable crops is "globalized by default," only being able to sell the results of a good or bad harvest according to international market prices, exporting tons of food and grain for industry via city brokers in London.

Whereas farmers are faced with these mammoth often overwhelming threats mostly on their own on a daily basis for years, tech venture teams are comparatively "lucky" in that you can rarely be a sole trader to launch disruptive innovations. That means you do need to find supporters and promoters—brand ambassadors—of your unique product or service beyond your "farm," incubator territory, and psychologically move out of your comfort zone faster than a typical farmer.

Tech entrepreneurs need to pitch their ideas to the world as soon as possible to test "market traction" and sustain that user uptake of their new SaaS product. Unlike most farmers—who only do "wholesale" and do not have any form of B2C trade like with a farm shop or a customer-facing retail business—tech venture teams have a direct interaction with their consumers and must face them fearlessly and ask for feedback, right off the bat.

The Case of the Medieval Sales Machine: Sir Loin Your Virtual Butcher

Paradoxically, on our family farm bordering Greater London in North Kent, we trialed a bespoke 2D chatbot in 2016 who could have become a revolutionary force in the global meat trade: Sir Loin Your Virtual Butcher.

Sir Loin, as in the meat cut sirloin, was named in honor of the Early Medieval Knight Sir Adam de Bavant, who was rewarded with our manor house and large estate after fighting the Scots on a crusade with the English king, Edward I. His Majesty was reputed to have also knighted a piece of steak, the tastiest part of beef, thus the English name sirloin steak. However, linguists also point to the French origins of the term as well *surloynge*.

In any event, we thought Sir Loin would attract a local Kentish following and explain the new products in the farm shop, such as environmentally friendly pasture fed beef and lamb, which was reared as grass fed only livestock by us. And then the chatbot could rattle off all the health benefits and pronounce that the healthier animals created a healthier, leaner meat for humans. Environmentally, it was better for sustainable farming by eliminating the need for grain feed that is required for animals we eat rather than human consumption. This archaic "traditional" farming practice takes up a lot of land as a global resource that could be more efficiently used for human food production.

Figure 1.3 Prototype avatar for cooking, preparing food, buying fresh food, and recipes. "Sir Loin Your Virtual Butcher." © Cliff Lee

Loads of complex facts to do with our farm shop and its new food lines were indeed successfully presented by Sir Loin in the form of an approachable chat on the farm website. He even conversed about my husband's Green Credentials as a No Till, that is, no plowing farmer who was reducing the carbon footprint and fighting climate change using alternative farming methods like cover cropping. Sir Loin was a hit—in Seattle, San Francisco, and New York. Not sadly in his target market: Londoners and the Home Counties where we could deliver fresh meat packages when ordered online via Sir Loin.

Our medieval Knight with a special trade got such a following in
the United States on Twitter that we actually met with a UKTI Export
Adviser about how we might export:

- Fresh mince burger patties (beef, lamb, and game/venison);
- Bags of homemade pork crackling;
- Frozen meat pies; and
- Pasties and sausage rolls.

all made by our Court Farm Butchery & Country Larder—to thousands of geeky IT nerds who had rapidly become fans of Sir Loin. The
British export advisers out of their depth and couldn't grasp how the chatbot had gathered these demographics and statistics.

They exclaimed how did we gather this data when "normally" you had
to do months of laborious research on the foreign market, the product
segment, hire marketers over there, travel to the destination country to
meet industry experts, join Chambers of Commerce to get introductions
to partners to help with importing goods into their markets, and ultimately spend a lot of time, resources, and money over at least six months
before trialing the export.

I tried to explain that Sir Loin was our special envoy who had managed to do a lot of that groundwork in a matter of weeks via chatting
online and using the "pull factor" instead of "push." In the end, there were
just too many UK export hurdles for shipping fresh produce abroad. We
had to abandon our plan to leverage sales from Sir Loin.

Sadly we had to switch off or deactivate Sir Loin Your Virtual Butcher
after just six months working on our farm's website. He wasn't on our
Facebook page because Messenger bots were not widely used or known
at the time. Merely as an online 2D chatbot, customized for our family
business as an SME, he was too controversial and "too clever." Too many
of the villagers, that is, our farm shop's regular customers over decades
were "freaked out" by this thing alive on their local farm's website. Some
of the feedback I got was "Is it going to steal my credit card details or
e-mail address?" and others told me they refused to talk with Sir Loin
because they simply weren't "computerized enough" and preferred to chat
with our human butchers whom they trusted.

Becoming an Advocate of Entrepreneurs

More often than not, an individual decision maker will not want to risk their own job "going in to bat" for an emerging tech entrepreneur. That is the bad news or worst case scenario for the entrepreneur. The "when in doubt do not purchase" mode kills off any turbo charged, hugely impressive sales pitch or carefully nurtured and immaculately conducted negotiation. There's nothing you can do about human psychological needs and instincts for safety and security: "I will do anything—or nothing as the case maybe—to not endanger my job or position."

The best case scenario is the opposite case: where an entrepreneur of new SaaS or innovative AI wins a corporate or government (internal) advocate who not only understands their USP and "cause" to bring this world-changing tech to market, but also undertakes to do that within their own company or organization.

These people are harder to find and engage for your entrepreneurial cause because once they get a reputation among startups in a city that they are "gate openers" as opposed to skeptical, unnecessarily negative gatekeeping guardians, then it is increasingly difficult for even the best ventures to get an audience with these perceptive, courageous individuals with vision and foresight.

The more robust entrepreneurs will court such decision makers vociferously seeing their opportunity to secure often multimillion dollar or euro contracts for their hard fought, preciously guarded portfolio of first-mover clients. Too many innovators falsely believe their uniqueness or genuinely "different" or more competitive / cost-effective software will "win" due to its merits alone.

Like with job applications and who gets the formal offer from HR, this is sadly not always the case. The best "interview performer" very often wins, much like the best performing "pitchers" of new ideas, whether they are genuinely new and unique, competitive, and productive or not. Be aware of this scenario and its pitfalls from the outset.

This is like enacting a play or drama over and over. The script is familiar—passionate, terribly eager entrepreneur, cool distant purchaser, months of information exchange, due diligence, and then the final yes or no, just for an (often unpaid) pilot of this emerging technology.

What Is Preventing Purchasers From Buying

Yet who wins this "do or die" opportunity may not always be the one deserving to win based on simple merits, due to a variety of reasons that I will explore in this book through case studies, commentaries, observations, and the guidelines at the end. A brief indication is:

- Purchasers not having the experience to distinguish hype from reality
- Not knowing where the correct or most relevant knowledge base can be found
- The independence of analysis fails due to "influencers" of the wrong kind
- Not being given the essentials of how to upskill themselves in a hurry to make an assessment of the proposal put forward by the tech entrepreneurs (the RFP or estimate)
- Not understanding that business chatbots basically fall into just two categories:
  1. Bespoke, boutique bot customizations created outside your company.
  2. "Off-the-shelf" bot APIs that are then tweaked and customized inhouse by your webmaster or a specially designated R&D team, often known as a greenfield project, with test implementation/deployment or pilot, for example, the summer 2019 Mixed Reality pilot of "Semmi" by Deutsche Bahn in the Berlin Central Station.

These issues remain a matter that must be repeatedly addressed openly and in a fearless way on a regular basis given the speed of scientific and technological advancements impacting on the whole world, not just your society, your city, your company, office, and ultimately, your job.

In conclusion, let's reflect on my definitions and observations from my 2016 article for the San Francisco tech news platform *VentureBeat*, cited earlier in this chapter. Why are chatbots disruptive? My VB article is still being read today because over three years on, things have not essentially changed! Why isn't everyone aware of the disruptiveness of chatbots? Why isn't every vertical deploying one?

One reason is that bot developers have become the arch enemy of the advertising industry, as I explored in my post about how the transparency of the user engagement metrics expose the lack of transparency in the legacy reporting schedules of the advertising middle men, the large and mid-sized media agencies who have tried to stop the advance of these independent customer experience measurements. Ultimately it will put them out of business if they cannot justify their multimillion ad spends with accurate, coherent tracking of sales leads to conversion rates, the demographics of the opted in consumers, and the outcomes of the incredibly lucrative digital out of home (DOOH) ad and marketing accounts they have held for decades for most brands you know.

Why the Advertising Industry Is Threatened by Disruptive Bots

Why don't the advertisers like us? Because of these key reasons:

1. We cut their profit margins.
2. We can deliver transparent metrics unlike most other forms of advertising.
3. The middle men known as media agencies or advertising agencies sell "ad inventory" to big brands and multinational corporations. More accurately they *buy* the digital ad space from providers such as DOOH billboards, Wayfinder, outdoor signage, and online platforms. And SEO native ad placements in real time.
4. Their profit margins have been cut by Facebook and Google, among other digital ad platforms like native advertising providers and auction places, because these U.S. tech giants do not need the middle men to sell their ad inventory.
5. The brands and businesses, company owners, and marketing directors can buy the ad space and campaigns direct from FB and Google, for example. Meanwhile the purchasing of FB campaigns has become ever more automated and user intuitive, so easy for an unskilled person to utilize. The service supposedly has transparent metrics.
6. I say supposedly because Mark Zuckerberg himself said at the FB staff pow wow in San Francisco a few years ago, confessing that their ad inventory sales system was not working.

7. Instead of trying to drive revenues through selling advertising space to small business owners and large corporations, FB would instead devote their resources to a far more profitable revenue stream from January 2017 onward: chatbots on its Messenger platform. And probably its newly acquired WhatsApp instant messaging app to assist in a near total monopoly of the new digital advertising, global landscape!

8. Microsoft's Satya Nadella followed Zuckerberg's chatbot initiative, declaring Microsoft Bot Network and its pervasive deployment of Cortana as the new world dominating B2C and B2B chatbot interface would be the new revenue stream to beat all others.

9. In fact, Cortana was deemed to become the world master bot for all other chatbots. Something that has not eventuated since these Microsoft and Facebook declarations in 2020 and unlikely to occur as these tech giants have failed to demonstrate true AI bot capabilities in the evident lack of user adoption of Cortana and the many Messenger bot flops.

Then 2017–2018 saw the hype slump to serious turnover "lows." Now at the end of 2019 we are seeing a hype cycle begin again. This is evident in all the trade show invitations that land in my inbox daily—an AI bot conference on somewhere in the world every month! 2020 will be a boom year and finally see the predicted trillion dollar growth, slowly but surely.

At last a more modest upswing in bot orders and sustained deployment of their avatars, not just online. Being confined to 2D online chats in the past were highly restrictive and actually prevented users adopting chat. It wasn't really conversational AI as it wasn't AI at all as I look at in Chapter 3 with the Japanese Hologram Wife.

Confidentiality Agreements Mean Fewer Case Studies

Several of these case studies are about competitors to the company I co-own. The rest are about the Mixed Reality 3D avatars created bespoke by our new tech venture in Bavaria, AI BaaS UG in Munich, as well as the frequently frustrating, "sales cycle" and long lead time situations we repeatedly found ourselves in with my predecessor 2D chatbot startup velmai Ltd in Devon, UK.

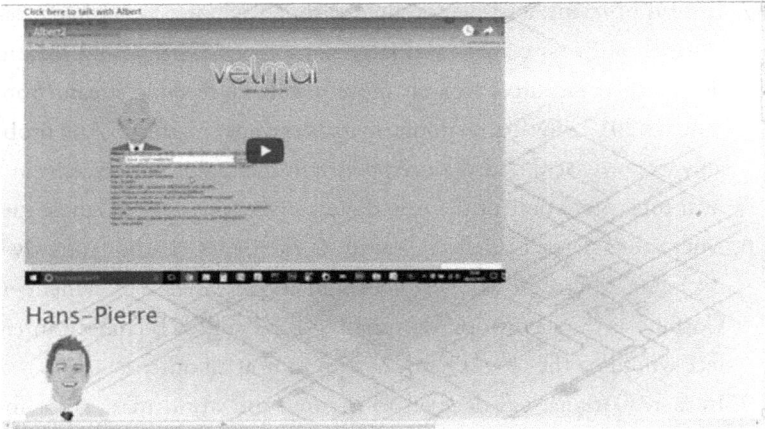

Figure 1.4 Most of our old venture's avatars were 2D chatbots that we deployed on websites and a few on Facebook Messenger for short experiments. Here you can see Albert the Online Butler who also switched to the author's Private Secretary using a wake word, plus Hans-Pierre who is a tourist guide and concierge working in tourist regions in DACH countries and the South of France. © Cliff Lee in Devon

Figure 1.5 Mixed reality installations are now at the forefront of point-of-sale user interaction, especially in large public spaces and where multilingual human–machine interaction is required to automate communications and enhance the customer experience. © AI BaaS Munich 2019

The reason for the few number of competitor case studies is that we are not privy to the production details, manufacture, and deployment issues of many of the "public cases" like Microsoft Tay.ai, Semmi, and Franny by Deutsche Bahn or the Labour Party of England and Wales. For the outsider, even for me as an expert commentator, we can only speculate as to why things go wrong for bot developers when they do.

Very few of them will ever release details or turn their pilot into a case study as I have done with my companies' projects here. For the tech ventures I have co-owned, I am able to publish details about problems in real-life situations, even where I have had to anonymize the client or facts and figures for the sake of our industry typical nondisclosure agreements (NDAs) and to ensure that our confidentiality agreements are kept intact.

CHAPTER 2

Most Young People Want Bots, Yet Purchasers Don't Buy Them

Chat apps have attracted billions of users, and bots are the mechanism that enable organizations to deliver highly personalized interactions at scale. Improved personalization delivers a more relevant user experience, and the high levels of automation used by bots enable cost-effective delivery at scale. As a result, businesses can engage with customers and achieve open rates that typically outperform e-mail and social networks.

Yet studies indicate corporate adoption of chatbots currently lags behind consumer openness to the technology, and that businesses would be wise to pick up the pace. According to a survey by Retale, "59 percent of US Millennials and 60 percent of US Gen X-ers have used chatbots on a messaging app" and chatbots have higher long-term retention rates than traditional apps. Yet Forrester reports that as of late 2016, only 4 percent of businesses launched a bot.

7 Reasons Why Corporate and Government Purchasers Should Deploy Bots

The best argument I have found was by the Canadian VC investment firm Georgian Partners, specialists in Conversational AI, based in Toronto. I am quoting them earlier from one of their many recent white papers on AI and (chat)bots. Georgian Partners has provided the best summary I have seen.[1]

---

[1] https://georgianpartners.com/investment-thesis-areas/overview-conversational-ai/

The figures are startling; if nearly 60 percent of U.S. millennials and Gen Xers have used them and want to keep using chatbots, then why don't we see 2D bots as an everyday tool, like a chat app? According to the Canadian bot analysts, 2D chatbot deployments and purchasing decisions accomplish seven key business goals:

1. One-to-one Conversation at Scale

   Leveraging automation, businesses can carry on thousands or millions of simultaneous ongoing chats using the app's native UX.

2. Personalization

   With a rich trove of data, companies can tailor messaging at the individual level based on interests, past behavior, and responses within the bot conversation.

3. High Engagement via Push Notifications

   Once positive experiences have been delivered, businesses can leverage push messages that go directly into user inboxes. Marketers, in turn, can rely on high open rates and an effective ongoing mechanism for re-engagement.

4. A Cure for the Brand App Blues

   ComScore reports that smartphone users spend 80 percent of their app time in only three apps. With multiple messengers topping app charts globally, having a piece of digital real estate on those platforms is an appealing alternative to building owned brand apps.

5. Revenue

   AI-driven chatbots can lead consumers through the entire sales funnel from awareness to purchase.

6. Efficiency and Productivity

   Bots have the capacity to enhance conversations between users by surfacing helpful information, or completing repeated tasks like scheduling.

7. Ambient Chat

   Major brands from GE to BMW are integrating chat functionality into Internet-connected devices, with bot technology powering those consumer interactions.

So given these seven brilliant reasons to buy a bot, what on earth is holding the purchasers back?

Appetite for Risk: Horses and Falls Versus Sharks and Yachting

What I have addressed previously is the appetite for risk of the entrepreneur somewhat obviously, and less obviously the risk-taking of investors in their invention or innovation (a lot of R&D needs premoney valuations to get make or break seed capital). Often overlooked are the risk averse tendencies of the corporate and government purchasers, perhaps because nobody wants to have the finger pointed at them, that is, blamed for a massive failure of the tech or perceived waste of financial resources, human resources, and time. Those with decision-making power are less likely to own up to their reluctance to take a risk seemingly on the behalf of an unknown tech venture.

Their risk assessment ought to focus on the "what's in it for me?" or my company/department. But these "value-add" points for their own workplace are sometimes forgotten postpitch and the purchasers return to their desk thinking, "What have I got to lose" rather than listing all the gains as a persuasive argument to put their bosses, peers, and colleagues.

Is there are risk to life and limb at the end of the day? It is highly improbable that you will lose your job if the greenfield project goes belly up. The much lauded tolerance of failure in the corporate world—though admittedly less so in government—is meant to kick in and the person who launched the pilot ought to be congratulated for their courage and fortitude.

An analogy is falling off a horse. As a teenager in Australia, when I was thrown off a galloping beast I decided to swap equestrian school for yacht racing. My calculation was that I could survive a shark attack if I fell overboard in the sea more easily than spinal injuries caused by horse-back mishaps. My appetite for (extreme) sports risks was balanced with a calculated assessment of the immediate threat or probability of injury if not a nasty death.

The point being corporate and purchasing decisions to support, trial, and pay for new technologies are simply not a life-and-death matter. So take your time to weigh up the pros and cons, the benefits versus the possible disadvantages a greenfield project or piloting of software could bring. What is the worst a customized, cybersecure AI bot could do to your department, company, or you?

The very worst case that you could lose your job is highly unlikely and if that came about, it says more about your employer than your capabilities. And the organization's appetite for risk and tolerance of failure is not where it should be. If it ever came to that, you ought to be working for more challenging, stimulating, and ultimately successful managers in the long term. If you can live with the improbable outcome of being sacked for a failed pilot and that is the only real threat prohibiting your attitude to experimenting with emerging tech, then you should take the plunge!

List of Regulatory Failures and Obstacles Blocking Bot Scaleups

- No regulation exists specifically for chatbots, AI bots, or botification.
- They are only affected via data protection laws and privacy breaches as guarded by the GDPR and similar legislation in other countries
- Even that remains a matter for enforcement, who has the onus of proof, who prosecutes and how—look at my analysis of the Tay.ai scandal and the Eugene Goostman hypedup claims in the next section to understand this better applied to clear international cases
- The laws and legislators have failed to address the issues that the Swiss Intervention was raising as discussed in my VentureBeat article "First chatbot arrest but what are the implications?":[2]

1. What happens when bots go rogue? How is going rogue defined under a set of international laws regulating botification?
2. Who is to blame when a chatbot does or says something illegal? As the Eugene Goostman debacle proves, liability is not clear given the apparent ignorance of the actual developers, a Russian and a

---

[2] Peitzker, T. 2016. "First Chatbot Arrest."

Ukrainian who had worked on the "chatbot parsing database since 2001" as to what purpose their chatbot was going to fulfill at the heavily publicized event in London while they were sitting in the United States and Russia; and how they and the bot were orchestrated by a PR-loving professor who had wanted to "win the Turing Test" for some time with earlier chatbot competitions staged by Kevin Warwick; the misleading statements of an unknowledgeable university marketing director who at first claimed they had created an Artificially Intelligent "super computer" (this was later corrected in a followup university press release from 2014, though they maintained that the Uni Reading event at the Royal Society had indeed passed the famed Turing Test as judged by a number of handpicked celebrities and well-known figures).[3]

3. If blame can be apportioned for the illegal actions of a chatbot or now a mixed reality AI bot hologram, how will the prosecutors produce evidence that may be hard to document on the web and also due to privacy laws preventing access to data and statistics such as User Experiences of the bot in question.

4. A lot is being published and debated about ethics in artificial intelligence. Yet why have so few AI ethicists given thought to chatbots? Perhaps because they have been maligned and obstructed, as I have argued in the previous chapter. Chatbots, for all their global influence and effect on companies' profits, have a still evolving though largely undocumented history.

Case Study #1 Microsoft's Rogue Twitter Bot and Trump Versus Clinton 2D Chatbots

The Microsoft Tay Hoax and Her Scarcely Known Successor Zo

This section is based on my 2016 *VentureBeat* article, "What to do when chatbots start spewing hate."[4] I wrote three articles for *VentureBeat* in 2016, as I wrote three posts for *Medium* in 2019.[5] A trio or series of blog

---

[3] https://reading.ac.uk/news-archive/press-releases/pr583836.html

[4] Peitzker. 2016. "What to do."

[5] https://medium.com/@taniapeitzker

Figure 2.1 © *Cliff Lee and Darren Lee in Devon. "Sophia the Market Researcher." The loss of trust in the marketplace was largely caused by the worldwide media coverage of Microsoft's Tay chatbot that went rogue*

posts for well-known tech news platforms was a good strategy for each set of circumstances at the time. Along the lines of less is more, I have kept my public profile pretty much under the radar, despite doing keynotes and talks at prestigious business schools and international conferences.

These days, as some sort of chatbot authority, I can summarize the Tay.ai incident as follows:

1. Tay was released by Microsoft Bot Network on Twitter, which in itself was strange because most chatbot developers (still) do not have access to the Twitter API. That means very few people can put a chatbot on Twitter independently of the company, which suggests that the Microsoft (referred to from here as MS) parent company did a deal with Twitter Inc.

2. What happened? The mainstream, largely uncontested story goes: Tay. ai was an innocent MS-owned chatbot demonstrating her supposed AI capacity with her own Twitter feed when suddenly she was "hacked" and/or "manipulated" by chatbot enthusiasts with malicious intent.

3. These malign "hackers" were solely responsible for corrupting Tay's innocence by "teaching her" bad things, racist concepts, offensive remarks like "feminism is a cancer," and worse, which I don't care to repeat here in this book.

4. If you search for "Tay chatbot" the headlines of the search results tell their own tale: the mainstream media and even a lot of tech experts promoted that idea that an essentially good AI bot had been tainted and corrupted by so called "evil, malicious humans."

5. Why was this untrue? Because there is no objective evidence this Twitter account was hacked and Twitter itself would have taken action to block the feed immediately if it had been.

6. Which begs the next question, why didn't the owners of the Twitter feed and the installed chatbot Tay block the account as soon as there was trouble? They could have easily taken down the account early on but instead they let it remain active, tweeting the most offensive remarks and retweeting comments for at least two days.

7. Seemingly enjoying the PR and marketing boon much like a Bad Boy YouTuber gets when an Influencer causes offense in the millions of views, Microsoft let Tay continue to "innocently" repeat the worst humankind had to offer, along the lines of Reddit and Breitbart styles of uncensored sewage of commentary.

8. Microsoft was not sued—at least not that we know of successfully— by any human rights advocacy groups, ethnic groups that were maligned or government regulators.

9. Their immediate "defense" issued by the MS Comms Directors was that Microsoft was an innocent owner of a chatbot that had been cruelly led astray and caused offense to millions of people—unwittingly because Tay was just a chatbot after all.

The glaring holes in this argument are as follows:

(a) Microsoft being a multinational multibillion corporation would have had staff watching this chatbot around the world, so all time zones in that first 24 hours of public-facing performance. Why on earth didn't one single Microsoft manager or staffer take the decision to banish the malfunctioning chatbot?

(b) It is relatively easy to build in defenses like filters to stop a chatbot, no matter how smart or dumb, from learning "bad words" and offensive ideas. That is Create a Bot Tutorial 101.

(c) It is even easier to switch off or hide a bad bot instantly. Hiding it is easy because you deactivate it in the account it is operating in, Twitter, Facebook Messenger, or Microsoft Bot Network in this instance.

(d) The killer evidence that quashes all of Microsoft's protestations of innocence and "lack of liability" for the chatbot's misdemeanors and crimes, for example, incitement to hatred and violence, defamation of identifiable groups and so on. is simply where is the good chatbot now?

(e) Microsoft did release a successor to Tay, and she was called Zo and lasted from 2016 to early 2019.[6]

Perhaps the AI capabilities of a Microsoft build chatbot never existed. Surely if Microsoft possessed the Holy Grail, the AI that all bot developers want to demonstrate, they would do so in the successor chatbots to Tay? But they have not, to this day in 2020.

It may well go down as the greatest deliberate hoax in chatbot history. It hasn't been called out by many of us, only a few brave tech bloggers like me. Because there is a lot to fear when a U.S. giant effectively rules

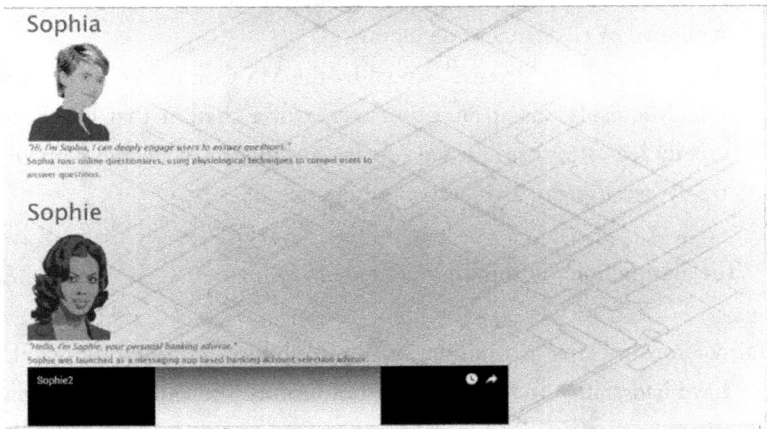

Figure 2.2 © Cliff Lee for the avatar UX and Darren Lee for the website graphic design. The financial Services 2D chatbot Sophie became hard to sell after the Microsoft "Tay disaster"

---

[6] Wikipedia, screenshot entry about Zo bot by Microsoft, accessed October 17, 2019.

the word processing world. And is part of a tech giant cartel that can distribute punishment as much as it can offer to merge and acquire you. The worst outcome was the fact it became very hard for many 2D chatbot developers to sell their independent services to prospective clients—they all lost trust in bot developers abilities to "control their avatars." If Microsoft couldn't control Tay, how can you control yours or stop it from being "corrupted"? It really damaged sales for many of us, in particular several challenger chatbots my old company velmai had released around this time.

The Clinton Versus Trump Chatbot Wars

I will keep this summary brief because it is fairly self-explanatory. If you search online (I recommend the search engines Qwant from France or Startpage.com from the Netherlands), then you will find secure independent results for this query "trump clinton chatbots." There is a plethora of blog posts and news items about the effect these avatars had on the last, highly passionate, and controversial U.S. election. Needless to say a lot of the spam bots against Clinton that ranted on Twitter and FB were guilty of hate speech, harassment, and ethnic vilification or incitement to hatred, automated or not.

The primary presidential contenders Hilary Clinton from the Democrats and Donald Trump from Republicans were neck and neck. Curiously this is the first time in global and chatbot history that two mainstream American political parties both and/or their supporters resorted to avatar deployment, even being analyzed and taken very seriously by the iconic, traditional *Washington Post*.[7] In fact, one bot developer SapientX created chatbots for both sides of politics simultaneously,

---

[7] Even at the start of 2018, *The Washington Post* reported on the latest AI bot attempt to recreate Trump in terms of an organically forming Markov algorithm – as the article shows, it didn't quite work which means the earlier standard NLP or NLU chatbots were actually better at rendering his personality as a 2D avatar for or against him. https://www.washingtonpost.com/news/politics/wp/2018/01/16/meet-trumpbot-the-bot-that-tries-to-talk-like-trump/?noredirect=on

presumably taking an unbiased Trump versus Clinton stance to get views and interactions of their tech.[8]

A *VentureBeat* editor was very impressed by the AskHilaryandDonald. com platform, which is now defunct if you try to click through by the way. Here is Khari Johnson's introduction:

> There may be an app and (pretty soon) a bot for just about every-
> thing, but this might be a first. SapientX, a company that has been
> in stealth mode for the last year, has created chatbots for Donald
> Trump and Hillary Clinton that provide words directly from the
> candidate's mouth on topics ranging from abortion to taxes and
> terrorism.
> The chatbots are able to answer questions in text or voice about
> roughly 100 topics, like: "What do you think about the Black
> Lives Matter movement?" or "Do you think that women should
> be paid as much as men?" A full list of sample questions and topics
> is available in a Venture Beat article.[9]

Interestingly though Johnson says SapientX has been in "stealth mode," they then quote one of the founders who says they have actually been operating sometime with "Conversational AIs" and voice-based chatbots—with no less than the U.S. Intelligence Agencies (CIA, FBI).

> The Hillary and Donald bots are SapientX's first publicly shared
> bots. Before launching these voice recognition political bots, Sapi-
> entX was working with "various departments of US intelligence
> on AI and bot technology for more than a decade," Hirshon said.[10]

---

[8] YouTube demo video of the AskHillaryandDonald chatbot platform by SapientX in the USA, https://youtube.com/watch?v=CzqTJYW-bTs&feature=youtu. be

[9] Johnson, K. 2016. "This Donald Trump Chatbot is Great... Really, Really Great. It's Unbelievable." *VentureBeat*, July 20, 2016, https://venturebeat. com/2016/07/20/donald-trump-hillary-clinton-chatbot-sapientx/

[10] Johnson, "This Chatbot is Great."

Johnson also mentions several other Trump Bot platforms that were caricatures or satirical spoof avatars functioning independently of the Presidential Candidate in 2016, a year after both he and Clinton announced they were running for the top job.

www.deepdrumpf.com was based on a satirical piece by the well-known British comedian migrant to the United States, John Oliver, in his *Last Week Tonight* weekly comedy show broadcast on HBO. Deep-Drumpf is a Twitter bot that became defunct (like many 2D chatbots that have gone to an early grave!) in May 2017, a bit over a year after it had its account created in March 2016. The avatar's Twitter feed profile states enigmatically, in an attempt to crowdfund its own existence:

DeepDrumpf

@DeepDrumpf
I'm a Neural Network trained on Trump's transcripts. Priming text in [ ] s. Donate (http://gofundme.com/deepdrumpf) to interact! Created by @hayesbh.

Another curious Trumpian avatar was *Donald Trumpbot*, which did not quite reach 900 followers and only had seven likes as a Twitter bot in just over a year's life as a NLP chatbot from 2015 to 2016.[11] The similarly defunct Trumpbot also sounded like it was hugely entertaining before it too was decommissioned by its satirically minded creators:

> Now, there are some important differences between Donald Trump and Trumpbot to keep in mind. There are the obvious ones, of course: Donald Trump is a 69-year-old business tycoon; Trumpbot is about 75 lines of code written in the Python programming language. Donald Trump is running to be president of America; Trumpbot is running on a server somewhere in North America. But there are some upsides to Trumpbot: Unlike the real Trump, it will never refuse to answer you (although it might change the subject sometimes). It will never demand $5 million for an appearance (although it can't actually appear anywhere

---

[11] https://twitter.com/thetrumpbot

except inside a webpage). And it will never release a strange letter from its doctor (it has no physical form and, subsequently, no doctor). Occasionally Trumpbot's responses have nothing to do with your actual questions. In that way, Trumpbot is certainly Trump-like.[12]

From what I understand, most of the Messenger bots were built for Facebook pages created and run by supporters of the Democrat and Republican political parties.

Another good example is an American media agency that created the BFF Trump satirical chatbot, admitting that it was biased in that it had "worked for the Democrat Party before." However, it is important to note that the two official chatbots created as political propaganda weapons for the Clinton campaign were developed by staffers with chatbot building skills in her office. A type of political intrapreneur I guess you could call this activity or job role.

[BFF Trump was a] Facebook Messenger bot that also sends you some of the most offensive things Donald Trump has ever said. The bot aimed at young voters was made by SS+K, an agency with a history of working with the Democratic Party. SS+K also redesigned the Democratic Party logo, according to Fast Company.
In recent days, BFF Trump has been one of the most popular bots on Botlist. Elana Berkowitz, creator of the HelloVote voter registration bot, has worked with the Clinton campaign, but both of the Clinton campaign bots were made in-house by the Clinton tech team, a campaign spokesperson said.[13]

I then read SS+K joined with Dexter to win over $2 million in Venture Capital to create a chatbot platform! The same source of this investment info, from the same VB report quoted earlier, also recommends the

12 https://splinternews.com/in-your-darkest-hour-you-can-talk-to-this-chatbot-vers-1793853587

13 https://venturebeat.com/2016/08/22/5-bots-to-try-this-week-bff-trump-futurestate-bits-sensay-and-the-fixer/

company FutureStates as a nonpartisan chatbot provider of politicians as interactive avatars, giving you sources for the policies they quote. Unlike many of its peers that only use basic NLP bot brains that recognize key-words, so they often give you wrong information for a query, for example, why don't you show us your tax records? With the response being a tweet or Instant Message about a tax policy instead.

Yet as you can see from the *BFF Trump* Facebook page here, it became deactivated very early on in 2016 and had less than 600 fans and follow-ers.[14] Given the aforementioned rapturous descriptions, you can see how easily one single chatbot can be hyped up just through a good-looking website, some established names, credible spokespeople, impressive mar-keting materials and some serious sounding reportage.

In my ABC Queensland radio interview in July 2019,[15] I refer to one of these official chatbot satires created by the Clinton campaign. What I explained live on radio was that someone was running a Donald Trump bot that was satirical as I only discovered this chatbot was an official party one while researching this book post Australian Broadcasting Corp interview.

The previous report by VB's Khari Johnson confirms this world first phenomenon of an official chatbot "strategically deployed" by a politician during a national campaign. Note the "Text Trump" chatbot we are going to look at more closely here was designed to live on the official www.hillaryclinton.com website not on social media. Like many of its chatbot cohort, it was a temporal avatar that has now been deactivated, that is, it no longer pops up on the Hillary Clinton site.

Johnson does a good bit of investigative reporting by getting state-ments directly from the source of the bot creation (thank you to VB's standards of reporting for the sake of tech posterity!):

The bot was highlighted in a tweet today by creator and Clin-ton campaign designer Suelyn Yu. It draws on the same backend database as Literally Trump, a hillaryclinton.com fact-checking

―――――――――
[14] https://facebook.com/bf=trump/
[15] See the News section of my portfolio site, www.ai-baas.com

page used during the first presidential debate, a Clinton campaign spokesperson told VentureBeat in an e-mail.[16]

Even more relevant to my other case studies in this book—on the UK Labour Party's Facebook Messenger bot that was cloned multiple times for (illegal) electioneering on a supposedly private dating site and the University of Kent internship challenge I created for on behalf of another British political Party—is the fact the Democrat's Campaign Office created a second electioneering Messenger bot to highly targeted, real vote conversion effect.

> The Clinton campaign also launched the I Will Vote Facebook Messenger bot today. It helps you register to vote or verify that you are registered to vote. It can also point you to your local polling station, and it says it can answer "any questions you have about voting." The bot was made by the Hillary for America tech team, said campaign CTO Stephanie Hannon in a tweet today.[17]

The example I often cite of The Donald satirical bot was that it scored policy points for the Clinton campaign by highlighting the most ludicrous or untenable claims of the Trump candidate vis-a-vis fact-checking live. It put basic natural language processing, botified, to a good search and find delivery use case. To summarize its success:

- When a user landed on the official Hillary Clinton website—of any political persuasion—they could opt to engage with the Text Trump avatar when the chatbot popped up. They could ask him questions, he would chit chat and be engaging while delivering Notable Quotes from the Real Life Trump on the campaign trail and links to policy documents or videos.
- If the user was slow in asking another question, then Text Trump would snappily text them saying, "Hurry up and ask

---

[16] https://venturebeat.com/2016/10/10/clinton-campaign-launches-bot-that-texts-you-donald-trump-quotes/

[17] Johnson, "Clinton campaign launches bot,"

me something or you are FIRED!!!" in true Trumpian, unilateral tweeting style as we've come to know and—for most of us—loathe it in terms of serious policy making and delivery for the common good.

Khari Johnson makes the point that Text Trump is really about Democrat fundraising, as the infotainment part of this clever 2D NLP chatbot leads to a conversion target or objectives for sign ups and real monetary transactions that all add up in a heated political campaign like the last U.S. election.

It seems that Text Trump was also operating as a Messenger bot on Hillary Clinton's Official Facebook page. As social media histories are still fairly ephemeral, we could only confirm this by contacting the journalist or the bot creators directly. As Johnson explains, "Eventually, the bot will ask you if you want to receive promotional SMS messages from the Clinton campaign or ask you to give $5 to the campaign."[18] Meanwhile many of the Clinton chatbots, run clearly by Far Right, Breitbart type enthusiasts or pro-Trump bot geeks, were clearly out to derail her campaign by redistributing slogans, anti-Clinton allegations, and policies designed to counteract the Democrats' positions.

On a closing note, there was an Obama Bot that was working officially on President Obama's government page in Washington for a while. If you read John Brandon's analysis of the Obama Bot in his *VentureBeat* opinion piece, he was quite scathing about its obvious limitations.[19] Brandon made a good case to show what I am arguing in this book: there are a lot of advanced bot technologies that have not gone to market because they were blocked as emerging tech.

Not to say that the Obama Bot deliberately stood in the way of its more disruptive and AI-capable cousins. However, as Brandon argues, the "safe choice" of a boring NLP chatbot that was repetitious in its servicing Frequently Asked Questions was a disservice to the chatbot industry. It

---

[18] Johnson   https://venturebeat.com/2016/10/10/clinton-campaign-launches-bot-that-texts-you-donald-trump-quotes/

[19] https://venturebeat.com/2016/08/14/the-president-obama-chatbot-on-face-book-messenger-is-an-epic-fail/

was historically the most famous chatbot—or *should* have been the most famous one—yet it is clearly forgotten in the wake of less capable but more notorious chatbots like Tay.ai and Eugene Goostman that supposedly had passed the Turing Test via an orchestrated attempt run at the Royal Society in London in 2015.[20]

Eugene Goostman Winning the Turing Test in 2014, a Controversy of Chatbot Hype?

Professor Kevin Warwick at the University of Reading had already run a Loebner Prize or Turing Test at his university in 2008 when Elbot from Germany and Sweden won.[21] Warwick has often been a controversial figure, for example, when he claimed to be the world's first cyborg as well! As I blogged at the time, the real fault was the media including the BBC for triggering a fairly intense, international wave of media hype with their unequivocal headline: "Computer AI passes Turing test in 'world first.'".[22]

Some brave bloggers and online tech news platforms like the *Huffington Post* and *Mashable* took a stand against the overstated claims and disputed that the Goostman 2D chatbot had passed the Turing test.[23] I also gave some off the record analysis to tech editors about this as I did not want to be seen as a competitor trying to take down the globally lauded achievements of several institutions, including the British Royal Society echelons, no less. It is needless to say how easy it has been to

---

[20] "The AI that wasn't" https://thedailybeast.com/the-ai-that-wasnt-why-eugene-goostman-didnt-pass-the-turing-test

[21] http://news.bbc.co.uk/1/hi/england/berkshire/7666246.stm

[22] https://bbc.co.uk/news/technology-27762088

[23] https://mashable.com/2014/06/12/eugene-goostman-turing-test/?europe=true Meanwhile, the HuffPost ran several articles as to "why Eugene Goostman passed the Turing Test": https://www.huffingtonpost.co.uk/jack-copeland/turing-test-eugene-goostman_b_5478112.html?ncid=other_email_o63gt2jcad4&utm_campaign=share_email; "Don't Believe The So-Called Turing Test Breakthrough" https://www.huffingtonpost.co.uk/entry/turing-test-eugene-goostman_n_5474457?ri18n=true ; "AI and EG: Why You Shouldn't Believe the Reports on Eugene Goostman," https://www.huffingtonpost.co.uk/thom-james/ai-and-eg-why-you-shouldn_b_5481466.html

hype advances in chatbot history, with a few famous names, for example, the celebrities roped in unwittingly who tested Eugene Goostman publicly—filmed for TV—at the Royal Society in London and run as a global Turing test to celebrate the birthday of Alan Turing, Britain's gift to the world of AI.

Germany's Reaction to the Political Chatbots and the Cambridge Analytica Scam

If you think I am exaggerating the effect of politically created chatbots on the last U.S. general election, then think again. Europeans watched in democratic, intellectual horror the supposedly entertaining advance of spam bots on Twitter—see the previous my discussion of Microsoft's Tay orchestration and how her successor Zo was so dumb she was deactivated in 2019 after only a few years in operation with comparatively few users and hardly any PR or tech discussion of Microsoft's "magic AI bot." The fact is, if Tay was so clever, how could her sister Zo be so ordinary and clearly just another NLP chatbot.

In the meantime, purchasers lost even more trust in bot tech. Spam bots, particularly the harassing sort on Twitter and Facebook or the annoying ones on Skype and kik.com, have actually wrecked the market for serious bot developers. That is until the year 2020 when the chaff has become separated from the hay, thus the rationale and timing of this book.

Looking back on the past decade that my 2D chatbot venture in Britain languished in a premarket, R&D phase, what were the repercussions for Internet regulation, privacy laws, electoral campaigning rules, and society's general well-being and satisfaction with the onslaught of fairly low performing, one-dimensional 2D chatbots on social media and websites?

The German Chancellor Merkel's reaction—supported by her even more Conservative Bavarian counterparts the CDU weirdly in unison on this with the Green Party of Germany and Die Linke, the far Leftists who were once the Communists of East Germany—was to suggest banning the social (media) bots that can influence an election. This policy if not legislation call was *before* the exposure of the Cambridge Analytica scandal and confirmation of Russian interference in U.S. elections by the CIA. British Intelligence and other sources have also indicated that the Russians did this (via Facebook advertising manipulation at the very least, with some evidence of politicized chatbots) in the UK general elections and of course, the deeply divisive Brexit referendum.

I discuss the aforementioned political events again in the afterword in Chapter 6. If you somehow missed the Cambridge Analytica global breach of privacy by misusing millions of people's Facebook data to politically target them, I strongly recommend you watch this Netflix documentary released in July 2019, *The Great Hack*. It is the best analysis and summary of the far-reaching dimensions of this scandal.[24]

The Great Hack falls short of showing the involvement of Cambridge Analytica's investors as being Brexiteers with a fierce agenda, as well as having investors in the company who were Tory MPs past and present, not to mention former Heads of Defense and other civil servants in Britain. This all came out in the subsequent flurry of investigative reporting into the overlapping interests and compromising political ties of a supposedly neutral, privately held data mining company.

The New York Review of Books journalist Tamsin Shaw concurs with me in this view. I spotted her review curated on the film criticism platform *Rotton Tomatoes*' page for *The Great Hack*.[25] Shaw is a friend and colleague of the British journalist at *The Observer* and *The Guardian*, Carole Cadwalladr. It was Cadwalladr who broke the story on Facebook's integral involvement in the Cambridge Analytica breach of personal data, subsequently suffering death threats, legal action by the named perpetrators. and ongoing misogynistic abuse.

As Shaw muses upon the release of *The Great Hack*, the real story was how billionaires and authoritarian individuals were attempting to undermine and control democratic institutions, not just breach the data

---

[24] Jehane Noujaim and Karim Amer, *The Great Hack*, documentary, Netflix, Released July 24, 2019.

[25] Review of The Great Hack, "Critics Consensus: The Great Hack offers an alarming glimpse of the way data is being weaponized for political gain -- and what it might mean for future elections." https://rottentomatoes.com/m/the_great_hack (accessed on October 19, 2019)

of billions of ordinary people like you and me to further their own power and reach:

> The bigger picture, which Carole and I had been discussing during those preceding months, was the way in which the Cambridge Analytica story opened a window onto a new constellation of international billionaires, corrupt politicians, and war profiteers who were apparently amassing enormous power. That story isn't only about technology, data, and psychographic profiling; it's also, at root, a story about the consequences of entrenched economic inequality, the privatization of essential public assets and government functions, including even national security, and the challenge to conventional foreign policy posed by the bargains being struck between international kleptocrats. And it tells us why, beyond being manipulated on social media, we should care about businesses like Cambridge Analytica—and why we should be concerned about what the Mueller investigation failed to expose.[26]

As the serious newspapers' reporting uncovered, there were two sisters on the board/investees of the now insolvent Cambridge Analytic firm, super-rich British Brexiteers who ran PR campaigns and worked closely with the key investor Stephen Bannon, a Koo Klux Clan support act at the Far Right American news platform *Breitbart*. Bannon of course was later belligerently famous as Trump's media and strategy adviser until he was unceremoniously kicked out of the White House, as have been so many of President Trump's dodgiest acolytes.

Off the record, I was interviewed by the Technology Editor of the Establishment, centuries old newspaper, *Die Suddeutsche Zeitung*, in Munich about the call to ban "social bots" in Germany when I was a keynote speaker at CeBIT Hannover in March 2017. He was making the case for Business Bots as opposed to the much feared "social bots" possibly about to be banned under German law as a danger to democracy if allowed to manipulate people during election time. Note the German

---

[26] Tamsin Shaw, "The oligarch threat," *New York Review of Books*, August 27, 2019, https://nybooks.com/daily/2019/08/27/the-oligarch-threat/

commentators combined the English keywords into "social bots" to discuss the phenomenon of manipulative, NLP 2D chatbots online, as opposed to a term they coined in English for German debates on this: "Business Bots vs Social Bots."

Incidentally, I have frequently been interviewed off the record by leading technology editors. Three times by the BBC to date, with the last in-depth interview being about "how does it feel to switch off or deactivate an AI bot that you have created?" That was for an in-depth report by Zoe Kleinman in London, who had already interviewed me live at an event with peers, the *New Yorker* "UTTR on Chatbots" conference in London.[27]

I have had several chats with BBC tech editor, Leo Kelion, in person at the Beeb's HQ in London, and over the phone on the subject of the Microsoft Tay.ai hoax. I think he had read my *VentureBeat* article on "What to do when chatbots start spewing hate?" which was critical of Microsoft's "bad bot goes rogue stunt." As explained in this chapter, Tay's antics had seriously damaged the market for us and all other bot developers. Purchasers simply didn't trust chatbots anymore, after all, if a Microsoft bot could get out of control, how could smaller companies manage theirs?

In this chapter and the previous one, I assessed the often kneejerk subjective reaction of purchasers when faced with decisions about unknown, "experimental" new technologies. In the aftermath of Tay.ai and the media storm that was hyped up around it, ignoring the tech bloggers flagging it was probably a corporate hoax, the risks implied in adopting NLP chatbots were assessed to be far greater than they actually were. It was clearly a case of "when in doubt, don't" and the prospect of potentially being eaten by sharks as a better alternative to breaking your neck while riding a horse did not assuage the corporate purchasers or the public sector procurement fears.

---

[27] UTTR October 3, 2017. Press release from New York, "New York, NY—Ticonderoga Ventures, Inc. announces that velmai's Chief Executive will speak at the UTTR Conference on Chatbots (http://uttr.com) on October 3, 2017 in London." https://webwire.com/ViewPressRel.asp?aId=213646 (accessed October 19, 2019).

Case Study #2: A World First Wayfinder AI Bot Hologram in a German Shopping Center

Our pilot in a Cologne shopping center turned out to be an adventure, quite a drawn out one, but a roller-coaster of successes and failures none the less! We made several errors of judgment rather than wrong design choices or flawed code. Our proprietary algorithm on our side was solid and performed robustly. However, we did not anticipate the glitches from the side of our partners, suppliers and client.

Without going into those mistakes and slip ups in too much detail, I will summarize here the objectives and achievements of this deliberately anonymized greenfield project with two leading property developers who shall remain unnamed for the purposes of this book. Nonetheless determined researchers can find out who they are if they look at my Research-Gate profile or the publicly accessible *Medium.com* posts I wrote at the time, including photos from our mall trial.[28]

My ResearchGate account and Medium author profile was set up to log the findings of our pilot after I was interviewed by academic researchers at Harvard, Yale, and Delft universities. The published photos and comments would help them to independently conduct their research and citing of my company in their work.[29] One of the Ivy League researchers considered our Amalia Prototype to already be in the league of Google Home and Amazon Alexa (I am under a confidentiality obligation so I cannot specify who from where). She told me excitedly, "What you are doing is completely different to all the other commercial trials!"

Perhaps due to the anxieties caused by emerging technology, we lost far too much time just negotiating the contracts with the clients and hardware supplier. The e-mail chains and chasing the stakeholders could take up over 20 hours a week of my time as CEO for months. We first pitched in Cologne in April 2018 and then after a series of vacations and absences

---

[28] https://researchgate.net/profile/Tania_Peitzker2 and the three posts about the pilot in Cologne: https://medium.com/@taniapeitzker

[29] Some other media interviewed us around the time included the San Francisco-based www.knurture.com 's www.outfuel.com publication.

for the decision makers, plus an unexpected replacement of the hardware supplier first chosen by our side, we finally executed 12 months later.

We began 2019 with a live demo livestreamed on the last day of January 2019 to the Applied Machine Learning Days at the EPFL in Geneva.[30] That demo was the sister bot Portia, the Conference AI bot hologram, whereas the bespoke Wayfinder bot was Amalia. You can view the three video captures taken from the livestream in January 2019 in the film section of my Amazon author profile page. Just scroll to the right to find the short videos of Portia in action.[31]

Note that these two hologram personalities, Portia and Amalia, were built on separate bot brains, with specific bespoke content. Portia gives keynote addresses to conferences and does Q&A with the audience and moderators, customized to the specific topic of the session and overall conference theme. Meanwhile Amalia's multilingual brain has been built to talk mostly about shopping centers, the bespoke list of retailers and services within a mall, and the customized content about that point of sale for brands as well as the city she finds herself in.

Preparing the Software, Hardware + Customization for the Multiple Client(s)

Picture this: as a startup that has been sitting on its R&D for 10 years, we were pretty keen to get this (fully unpaid and entirely at our own cost) pilot underway. Off the back of this world first Wayfinder, we hoped to attract a whole lot of replica sales, the well-known multiplicator effect in sales and marketing. That was a calculated risk and investment on behalf of velmai Ltd in the UK.

Then visualize the harsh realities: me spending six weeks away from my Kentish home in my German family's holiday apartment in Bonn's Bad Godesberg, so I could do the two-hour commute each day by tram directly to the door of the shopping center in Cologne. As we had absolutely no cash coming in, only a lot of it going out plus all the sweat equity of our programming, bot coaching, customer liaison, client coaching, and

---

[30] https://appliedmldays.org/women/tania-peitzker
[31] www.amazon.com/author/taniapeitzker

partner relations, there were very few choices as to how to execute this with a zero budget. Self-financed or bootstrapped goes without saying!

Sales and marketing were actually taken care of for free with a Google Maps Local Tour Guide account for our twin bot Amalia and Portia. She started posting photos of her arrival in Cologne and attracted thousands of views within a matter of weeks! This evident curiosity for the deployment of new tech was reflected in the comments and engagement of the shoppers when she was finally released into the public space of the mall, being located in the center of it right by the escalators and across from the elevators.

In short, with a long commute to the client site up to four times a week for nearly two months, this was a heavy investment of time, money and energy on velmai's part in order to get the prototype up and running in a public space. The things that needed to be trained on site in German for the bot brain were the following:

- It had to be tested for the "map knowledge" of its surroundings, so the 30+ shops and facilities, restaurants, cafes, and services. Her overall performance with this was excellent, as I documented it here in my Medium post at the time.[32]
- Amalia needed continual practice—on site in a quiet office space above the mall—to understand the new information and random greetings and ways of addressing her in German only in real time.
- She needed to speak with Native Speakers of German because my German is spoken with a heavy English accent. That confused her and she kept replying to me in English, though she had understood my questions and comments in German![33]
- Some information we had (not) been given by the client had to be added at the last minute, for example, the underground floor was called Basement in both English and German, and

[32] https://medium.com/@taniapeitzker/when-hardware-meets-software-with-global-citizens-in-between-232d4ae78f85
[33] https://medium.com/@taniapeitzker/my-ai-bot-inferiority-complex-our-avatar-is-smarter-than-me-e97e5df35cfa

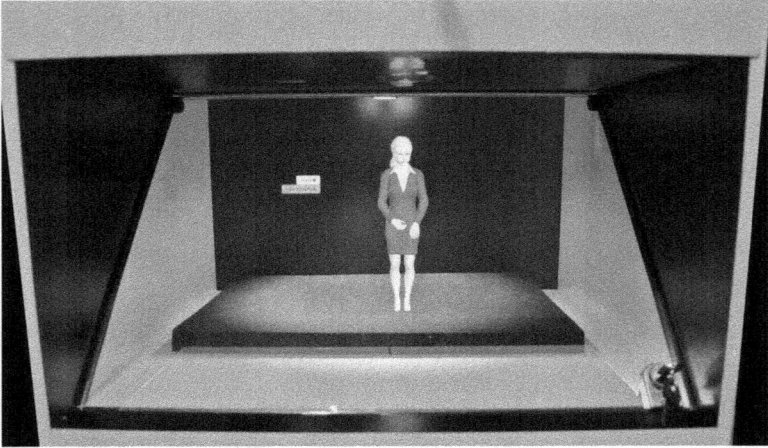

Figure 2.3 © *AI BaaS UG, Munich, 2019. Amalia I was deployed in a shopping center in Cologne with 10 million shoppers per annum. Here you see her successor Amalia II about to be deployed in Munich to small and large crowds for multilingual automation of Frequently Asked Questions and Infotainment*

they used the foreign English word for Untergeschoss. So that had to be tweaked for all the shops and food court eateries as well as the loos and baby changing room, plus the exit to the subway.

- The subway had to be referred to as the underground train or tube because the food outlet Subway was also located in the Basement. This confused Amalia's organically learning bot brain! As did other company brand names in English, for example, Flying Tiger Copenhagen, "Only" (a clothes store), Depot, the beauty chain store "Rituals," Comfort Baby, Claire's, Hair Express, the Barber, US Nails, Bun n Roll and Fruit World.

- I wrote a particularly funny piece about Amalia making jokes about the Iris Photography shop called Eyesight in one of my three Medium posts about this.[34] We had to change some of the entries like the iris photography shop which we humans had

---

[34] https://medium.com/@taniapeitzker/mixed-reality-offline-online-x-hybrid-existence-ebd02a08d42e

wrongly thought was an optician selling glasses and eyewear. In fact, it was a gift shop that Amalia ended up giving a lot of reflective thought to and making an unwitting joke out of.

Lessons Learned From a Business Development and Client Liaison Angle

What we had discovered in our trial in Cologne was

- Don't be too ambitious—as a Minimum Viable Product (MVP), the bells and whistles *must* come later.
- If the client insists on certain features that were not agreed upon in writing, then you can work out a timeline for adding those elements on at a later date, for example, in the next phase of the pilot.
- Control the client's expectations before, during, and after the implementation.
- Only work with reliable suppliers of hardware or any other external module you need.
- Off-the-shelf software plug-ins are easiest to add rather than getting bespoke coding done by partners.
- Bring it all in-house as much as possible! Then you are no longer vulnerable to the failures and lateness—including repeated delays and delivery of faulty equipment—of external suppliers and third party partners.
- We now send a client a template for the customization that must be filled out before we start building the bespoke bot brain. See our new company AI BaaS UG's standard template for clients in the following case study about Car Showrooms.
- We now have a standard contract that must be agreed and signed before we commence any type of pilot or corporate campaign. This stipulates payment terms and delivery milestones for all those concerned.

To date, nearly all hologram projections you see around the world do not have an AI bot brain. That makes AI BaaS UG the first bot developer globally to create a Cognitive Interface with voice via a hologram.

Figure 2.4 © Realfiction, Copenhagen, 2019. This Danish company is our hardware supplier and has been creating high grade "pre-recorded" holograms for nearly a decade. Their 3D holograms have limited interactivity, usually through a keyboard, buttons in the device and/or gestures

Case Study #3 A "Meet and Greet" Sales Hologram in Car Showrooms

This is a Request for a Proposal that our production and sales team were working on at the time of my completing this book, in autumn 2019. I will report on it in the next edition of this textbook, if not as a sequel or an article in a relevant journal. After we ran the shopping center bot hologram installations, our sales team decided the best next prototype in our pipeline would be a car showroom mixed reality installation. Unlike the shopping center AI bot hologram, this creation would do less Wayfinding and more direct selling.

To be installed at a point of sale, this means that the AI bot must understand tentative enquiries, hesitant questions about stock and inventory, and not being too pushy when it comes to the bot suggesting that the prospective customer speak with their human colleague. Obviously to progress the sale to a deal stage.

Our sales team need to manage expectations during the sales process so the client and other people in their organization mistakenly believe

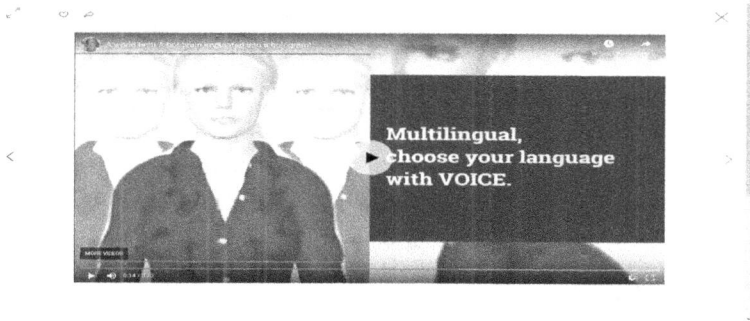

Figure 2.5 © AI BaaS UG, October 2019. Screenshot of our promotional video on our company landing pages www.ai-baas.com. The new venture launched from the Bavaria Film City suburb of Gruenwald in Munich in the autumn of last year

they have just ordered a humanoid robot or an AI clone like from a science fiction movie. Of which there are many to confuse and overhype what "The Uninitiated" in AI expect from our inventions and creations! For that reason, we have started creating demo videos and will have our prototypes operating live on various sites in Germany. If the prospect cannot travel to our host or showroom in Bingen am Rhein or on the Cote d'Azur, then they can participate in a livestreaming session with the AI bot hologram in both 3D avatar form and chat with its 2D self.

Case Study #4: UK Labour Party Bot Goes Rogue on a Dating Site

During the national general election in 2017, the UK Labour Party used a bespoke Facebook Messenger chatbot to devastating effect. I have used this example as an Ethics Test during my internship program that I have run twice now at the University of Kent in Canterbury. The international and local students who were our velmai interns for two weeks only were delighted by this challenge of "Dos and Don'ts" when creating chatbots for any purpose.

Essentially, the Labour Party created a chatbot on their official Party Facebook page. This meant that when you visited the UK Labour Party FB page during that election campaign (it was later deactivated), even without being a fan or member, you would be greeted by their avatar, which happened to be the English Rose, the logo of the party. I really should have taken recordings and screenshots of this phenomenon, as this little bot was to become quite historic in global chatbot evolution though the history may not have been written yet.

My case study for the Employability Points interns at the University of Kent was a first step to discussing the implications of this political deployment of a bespoke Messenger chatbot in Europe. The 2D chatbot was there to "meet and greet" visitors to the page. It did that quite successfully though I recall my conversations with it tested its limitations. For example, after saying hello and welcome, it launched into policy recommendations and news flashes. So far so good, but that can be repetitious for a supposedly "spontaneous," organic conversation between bot and human in real time.

Nevertheless, this little NLP chatbot, despite its content and conversational limitations, became a huge contributing factor where the Labour Party increased membership to record numbers, by the hundreds of thousands no less. Sure a lot of that was face-to-face campaigning by a leftist youth movement called Momentum, as well as the British Union Movement. But what has been overlooked to date in this electoral period of British history is how the bespoke Messenger bot increased the FB numbers on their FB page.

I am not privy to those statistics but I witnessed an increase through use of their FB page several times over a period of months during the election campaign. Purely out of professional curiosity to see how the brave NLP chatbot was doing as a Messenger bot amid heated political controversy. Also overlooked and representing a huge ethical controversy in chatbot history is the fact that Labour supporters and/or members replicated this English Rose logo avatar on Facebook. They then deployed this 2D chatbot on a dating site, without a logo or avatar, just a multitude of people's real names, as I explain in the following.

The controversy lies in the fact that:

(a) This chatbot took on various personas or the names of real people who were members/supporters of the Labour Party.
(b) The various personalities of this chatbot with real people's names were then given a variety of different personal addresses and post codes. Why?

(c) Because the dating deployment was a highly strategic, innovative campaign method to win swinging voters. How?

(d) The various clones of the Labour Party avatar were deployed in swinging electorates or townships/regions where Labour could win a marginal seat away from the Tory Party. Their professed fake addresses enabled them to contact single men and women "looking for love" on this dating app.

(e) The problem? The issue is that these lonely (human) hearts did not know they were being contacted by a chatbot, let alone a politically repurposed 2D bot who had the sole aim of influencing their particular vote in this hotly contested general election.

(f) How did the cloned, multiple personalities Labour bot accomplish this? It sent out automated text messages to its human targets on the dating site, asking them in colloquial informal and very convincing English "dialects" or slang "How are you going to vote today love? I'm for Labour!" And similar messages.

(g) The killer deployment or dating message by this politically motivated chatbot with numerous IDs so evidently a Multiple Personality Disorder executed on the dating site was a text the day before polling day. "Don't forget to vote honey!" and the like.

We don't know or have the actual metrics of the success rate or conversion rate of the bot missives to human lonely hearts. All I can say it was obviously worth the ethical and legal risk the bot managers took to do this!

Because no formal case study exists on this episode to this day, I got my interns in their busy two-week program with me to look into it, if they had time. We saw that the dating site company that had supposedly unwittingly hosted this caprice and had made a public statement about it with an online press release at the time.

They regretted that their users had been used like this by Labour Party supporters. They were investigating the incident and were taking action. I don't think they ever did. The Labour Party of course distanced themselves from the whole botified online shenanigans and said it wasn't the Party Head Office, administrators, or members, just some fans who got carried away online in their zest for a Labour win.

CHAPTER 3

Use Cases of the Best Practices and Worse Case Scenarios

Defining a Cognitive Interface by What It Is Not; the "Japanese Hologram Girlfriend"

I created this case study for a large audience of MBAs and staff at Cambridge Judge Business School in autumn semester 2017. I won't repeat the case study in this book because it is freely available online as a podcast on YouTube accompanied by the visuals in a SWAY PowerPoint.[1] The essence of the analysis was that the interactive hologram created by Gatebox in Japan was not a cognitive interface. It does not grow or learn. It is an excellent, high-grade animated 3D avatar.

The Hologram Girlfriend ever deployed in a small semitransparent cylinder for B2C use or mass consumption, to date largely in Japanese though there is uptake for her English version in the United States. However, the personality contained in the box is not an AI bot hologram as it is on a loop or repeated content. It doesn't learn from its owner or from interactions with humars to expand its repertoire.

Having said that, its performance as a standalone 3D hologram satisfying the needs of a particular market segment is remarkable. Its best innovation, rewarded with a fairly quick M&A takeover by a larger corporation in Tokyo, is the Hologram Girlfriend's success in being an IoT device in home environments, connected to the owners' appliances and

---

[1] "Dr. Peitzker on AI Bots at the University of Cambridge Judge Business School (55 minutes)",
128 views, October 21, 2017, https://youtube.com/watch?v=f2seNpAnlEs

being able to text him via his smartphone, a NLP chatbot in 3D communicating as a 2D replica with her owner.

It may be the subject of another book to look at chatbot history by continent, for example, in Africa, Asia, India, Australia,[2] the Americas.[3] We have had RFPs from South America and we noted that the most popular instant messaging app there is Telegram, which is also running thousands of interactive, basic NLP chatbots for a variety of use cases.

I stumble across Japanese, Korean, Chinese, Indonesian, Malaysian, and Singaporean chatbots constantly, not to mention the thousands coming on the Indian market. Many have been around for decades, like these corporate use cases for 2D chatbot applications via instant messaging platforms by a South Korean AI company that was established in the early 1990s.[4]

Eight Use Cases for Industry Verticals

For our marketing collateral, my company AI BaaS defined the following use cases:

1. Wayfinder and infotainment at malls, airports, train stations, and sports stadiums including sponsored marketing targeting "want to know" users during their chat sessions with velmai AI bot holograms on site in 3D multimedia format.
2. Conferences and trade shows—see the Portia experiment. Saves time, money, and energy when you can send a bespoke 3D hologram avatar instead of staff! She made a speech to AI experts at AMLD and took questions from the floor. The hologram can then be installed at the event for further one-on-one interactions.

---

[2] https://thenextweb.com/artificial-intelligence/2017/03/24/say-hello-to-nadia-the-terrifyingly-human-chatbot-with-emotional-intelligence/ On the Australian Chatbot market growing https://chatbotslife.com/revealed-the-top-5-hottest-chatbots-in-australia-70b73e0d9f02

[3] American Government chatbot examples https://chatbotslife.com/4-government-agencies-using-chatbots-faf98702b775

[4] https://estsoft.com/service_chatbot.html

3. Tourist guide and hotel concierge—similar to use case 1 but more bespoke content answering the FAQs of hotel guests and destination marketing goals.

4. University campuses for security and timetabling queries regarding room changes in real time. 3D is a mascot of the university that we can grant student teams access to, that is, they can upload new info via a CRM. The 2D replica can disseminate this via the university's and student clubs' social media pages. We have also been asked to do a Student Welfare bot for psychological support on campus.

5. Government departments and NGOs: again as Infotainment Wayfinder on site in large government buildings and spaces. 2D bots for B2C interactions and customizations to bring government services to life in real-time conversations to get bureaucracy done.

6. Point-of-sale sales assistants in store or for special promotional events—the 2D replicas on social media and the corporate websites reinforce the sales work and interaction of the 3D hologram AI bots live on site.

7. Marketing avatars for example at banks, insurance companies, and other services that have cut back on sales and reception staff. But as the first point of contact for clients, business partners, and suppliers, a 3D AI bot hologram on site is a 24/7 ambassador that can bring the IoT of the firm and the essential info together in "one brain."

8. Education generally: we have had many RFPs for tutor bots, for example, at MOOCs.

RFP Case Studies for "Dos & Don'ts": Hypotheticals Based on True Events

Case Study #5: Diplomatic Mission's Facebook Page and Messenger 2D Chatbot

This deal came about after a call from or to the Deputy Ambassador of an Embassy in London. (I can't recall how this RFP was initiated exactly). They wanted us to solve a political, technical, and social problem. Curiously, it was to do with Brexit and populism.

Without giving too many details, we can say that this entity ran a Facebook page that had thousands of fans visiting it regularly. At the time we drew up our proposal, there were 4 or 5,000 fans or followers on the FB page). Sadly, that number included numerous trolls and a few very aggressive Brexiteers who saw a conspiracy in everything.

So our task was to build a Facebook Messenger bot tailored to the mission statement and purpose of the page. It was to meet and greet the visitors in real time, for example, "Hi Thanks for visiting our FB page. How are you? Can I help you with information?" And then a tree structure with "pick your answers" that would graduate to a free form or unstructured response of the bespoke bot replying "naturally" to the spontaneous comment or question.

The main task, however, was for the bot to solve the problem of constant, random trolling of the site. The challenge was for it to identify abusive language and give automated warnings 24/7. The idea was to take the heat out of the escalating "discussions" among the "fans" of this FB page by having a calming, neutral, and "diplomatic" bot take care of basic communications without being provoked, angered, or upset by any personal attacks or verbal abuse by the visiting, "hostile" Facebook users.

It would have been the perfect case study to show how even a basic messenger bot could defuse hate speech online especially on Facebook, which is notoriously slow to remove offensive comments. Despite the platform making billions in profit a year in every corner of the globe, Facebook remains unable to deal with or police the nasty perpetrators of bullying and trolling.

Again, almost de rigor, we were about to start building this bot after it got sign off from all the stakeholders. Then Brexit took a bad turn and it was evident that those involved would have to change their policy and wind up this Facebook page as an "outreach" or PR project in the UK. The client could not justify the budget of £10,000 for the final 12 months of this online campaign before they were obliged to wrap it up, due to political changes and social pressures regarding the viability of running the project amid the furor of populist beliefs, unproductive negotiations, and the British public's escalating anger or frustration, as is the case now on the October 5, 2019, a matter of weeks before the Brexit Deal—or not.

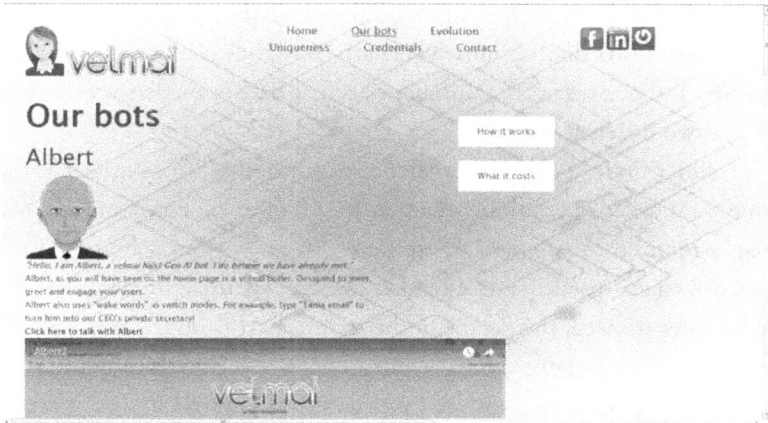

Figure 3.1 © *Cliff Lee, CCO from velmai Ltd. "Albert the Online Butler" (an iteration of Batman's butler Alfred) was the prototype that attracted the attention of this client in London. Albert was also voted the best innovation at the London Digital Travel Summit in 2017. https://youtube.com/watch?v=6coVEQzE27A*

Our chatbot company had invested time in face-to-face meetings and PowerPoints tailored to the goals and objectives of the job. The 10K was not the decisive factor for us; obviously a first mover client of this stature would have been a boon beyond the initial revenues! I later turned this proposal or request for a proposal (RFP) into a live case study for my Masters of Science students at an international business school in the south of France.

The challenge was to revive the project with other branches of this diplomatic envoy and organization in other countries. The course was on "Negotiations and the Use of CRMs." It turned out to be a very productive use of the students' imaginative ability to put themselves in the role of the entrepreneur and the nongovernment or NGO decision makers. They nearly closed two deals in Germany and Italy, with several other pitches drawing positive feedback and scoring a won deal by the end of semester, which they dutifully tracked in their ERPs in the cloud.

Case Study #6: International TV Station and Digital Broadcaster: Online Bot as Infotainment

This deal was won in a strangely "covert" way, without pitching directly for it. Instead we were unwittingly put into a "live experiment" and then chosen from our peers! We had received an invitation from New York for a one-day closed door seminar on chatbots with leaders from our competitors and our peers. The number of actual BaaS providers was limited to just two dozen at the most.

I didn't understand the conference organizers' business model at the time. As a one-day Londoner seminar for 20 of my competitors and less than a roomful of attendees, there were also no obvious sponsors of the event. Business participants attended for free, on the entrepreneur side. As we later realized, the people in the room, apart from the BBC, which interviewed me and two others on our AI bot panel in the afternoon, were from big corporations. They were purchasers or buyers.

Clearly, they were paying to "go undercover" to see us perform in our natural environment as was later explained to me by several HR experts. They had seen parallel practices in their fields obviously. Some of my peers unwittingly discussed big flops of bot deployments and failures in delivering, believing we were all there as BaaS providers.

The attendees did not have name tags and I only found out where some of them were from over lunch. I luckily landed on the table with the TV corporation that later gave me a call. It was between us and another company regarding winning the purchasing contract!

We were asked to quote on:

- A 2D bespoke bot.
- It was to do be a type of menu bot that helped users navigate the content of their online sites.
- It was the beginning of on-demand service in the UK and this corporation was already at the forefront for certain verticals.

The Pitch and Outcomes

In response to the stated needs of the client outlined mentioned earlier:

- We created a name and character for the avatar which his team liked.
- However, the marketing director was afraid of the bot's automation and typically for marketing and business development

(biz dev) people, thought there was an in-house plot afoot to undermine their authority and control of the site.

- The content had millions of users globally and we agreed to limit a first deployment to Europe only.

This was suddenly called off, after we had gone to the effort to send them a bespoke licensing agreement. The TV company did not replace us with a competitor bot. To my knowledge, there is still no botification of this site or any of the content available online.

The only clue we had to yet another cancellation preproduction was that the Project Manager who had engaged with us over lunch, actually a senior executive, had been seconded suddenly to another country and there was "new management" in the UK subsidiary. They were not open to continuing discussions of bots and botification to support users to find content on their site.

It could have helped users to locate videos and films they wanted to view. More importantly, it could have promoted and publicized content

Figure 3.2 © *Cliff Lee in Devon. "Charlie the Spoof Newsreader" was a prototype 2D chatbot for this content managing bot that was to promote the shows and topical documentaries online and also conduct "mini polls" and user quizzes on behalf of the brand or client*

they were not going to discover on their own. Being an in-house trusted corporate publicist, on-demand 24/7 in any language would have sent hit rates and user engagement skyrocketing.

Yet again, internal politics and problems at a global multinational corporation led to the obstruction of low-cost innovation and the delay of this emerging tech adoption.

Case Study #7: An Internationally Franchised TV Show: 2D Search and 3D AI Bots

We won the invitation to pitch for this TV deal, similar to the other on demand one discussed in this section, in an unexpected way. I had given a guest lecture at the prestigious Cambridge Judge Business School. It was announced as a talk on AI bots from an industry perspective. And the next thing I knew there was a huge queue to get into their biggest auditorium, with students having to sit in the stairwell and stand in the aisles.

After I spoke for nearly an hour on the Japanese Girlfriend and botification generally (see my discussion of this in Chapter 1), someone who had RSVPed but could not attend in person met with me one-on-one in Cambridge. They worked at a famous broadcaster and within a month or two, we were having a meeting with the Executive Producers of this nationally well-known TV show, which was also available online.

They had spent a lot of money on Amazon Alexa *skills*.[5] And they wanted us to fix them because they weren't really working to their satisfaction. The growing customer, user, and developer dissatisfaction with the product and bots as a service is relatively easy to find in (ironically) critical reviews on Amazon.

---

[5] There are endless sources of "how to" create botified experiences on Amazon Echo devices, known as Alexa (the Virtual Assistant with a multilingual voice) and the interaction or cognitive interface experience is branded by the corporation as a "skill." There are thousands of programmers, self-taught coders, and business Development gurus who have published manuals and instructions on this for other bot developers to join the army of Amazon Alexa Skills builders.

127 customer reviews

MR G S BOOTH
2.0 out of 5 stars Waste of money
July 13, 2018
Format: Paperback Verified Purchase
This really is a waste of money—it's easier to find much more info on the Internet. Why Amazon cannot produce a proper Manual (including all the commands Alexa can understand) along with complete instructions as to how to set up all the built in skills beggars belief. Finding out for example that after setting up a free Spotify account, it isn't until you try and link it that you are told it must be a paid premium account. This sort of time wasting is infuriating.
37 people found this helpful

Review of an Amazon Echo book on how build Alexa Skills.[6] I discuss the problems arising socially and psychologically with the mass uptake of Amazon Alexa globally in Chapter 6, in the conclusion and afterword of this book.

The *skills* that had been taught to the Alexa platform were meant to give search results from their massive archive via voice queries. However, the Amazon API and bot development was having trouble:

(a) Understanding the voice queries;
(b) Responding appropriately; and
(c) Finding the correct results.

One of the biggest problems was that to create the *skills* and then correct these issues was taking a lot of time, more human resources than they

[6] https://amazon.co.uk/Amazon-Alexa-Ultimate-Skills-Including/dp/1977082
734/ref=asc_df_1977082734/?tag=bingshoppinga-21&linkCode=df0&hvadid=
{creative}&hvpos={adposition}&hvnetw=o&hvrand={random}&hvpone=&hvpt
wo=&hvqmt=e&hvdev=c&hvdvcmdl={devicemodel}&hvlocint=&hvlocphy=&
hvtargid=pla-4583863980693737&psc=1

had anticipated and wasting a lot of time of their TV production crew and back office. That was not what they had bargained for when paying for this development. And then paying more again to fix the problem.

Why were we offered the job and then it was rescinded within a week? Because they didn't want to pay us because we were a no-name startup. We were meant to fix Amazon Alexa skills for this famous TV show for *free* and then go on to provide our better-performing AI bot with full integration into their archive and database of search results/user demanded content *for free*. Of course we said no. No, we didn't want the fame of working without pay for a famous TV production. Global or not. No thank you.

Case Study #8: Chamber of Commerce 2D Chatbot for Membership Recruitment

Again I am not sure which side initiated this first. I think we were interested in becoming members of this chamber. Then the CEO became personally interested in our technology, pilots, and innovation. We became his protege project within the organization for at least 12 months leading up to the U.S. elections at the end of 2017.

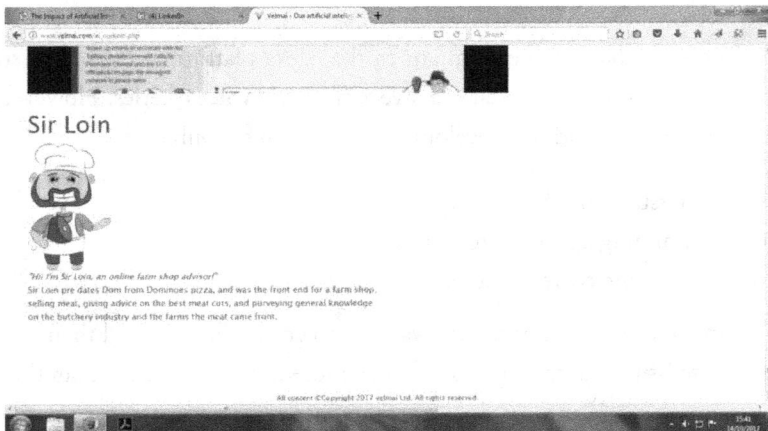

Figure 3.3 © Cliff Lee. "Sir Loin Your Virtual Butcher" and several of our 2D chatbot pilots inspired the prospective client to ask us to "fix Amazon Alexa" because the food-related "Skills" were not working. See Sir Loin's avatar in my Introduction which discusses this "alternative farm butchery and sustainability comms" case study

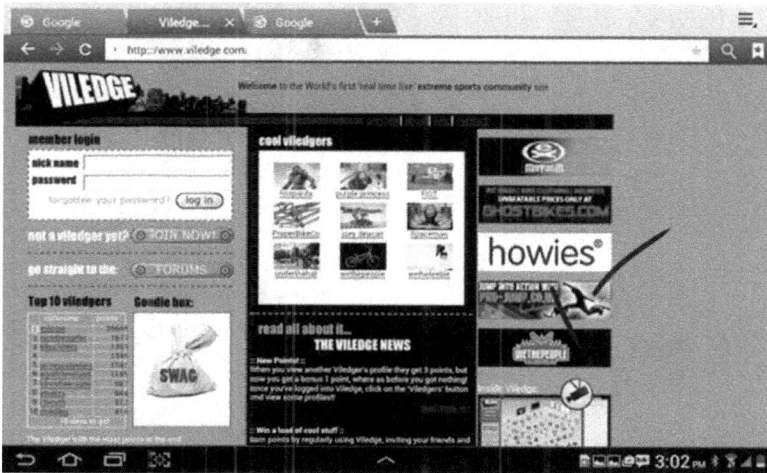

Figure 3.4 © *Cliff Lee, cofounder of viledge Ltd. This was the prototype startup before velmai. It was a social forum before social media i.e. before Twitter, chat apps and Facebook. Its purpose was remarkably similar: to connect people with each other through the use of "undercover" or incognito 2D chatbots. We were pioneers in deploying online bots who texted each other and the human members on the site, recruiting user numbers into the tens of thousands all on their own, without disclosing themselves as chatbots*

In one way, this was an incredibly simple bot to build, and in another, it was hugely challenging in terms of stakeholder interests! It took over a year to negotiate due to us being put in a role of service provider with special privileges. For example, we were going to be used as an exemplary proponent of chatbots in business. This would lead to us running a forum and networking group within the organization for members to explore notification, not just with us obviously but with all service providers.

We were about to create this female avatar who was to be the website's meet and greet bespoke bot. Her primary purpose was to recruit new members and also keep existing members abreast of events and initiatives. What happened? Without giving away the name of the longstanding entity, I can only say that a monumental election took place in their country of origin. From one month to the next, the CEO was replaced. Most of his team was sacked. And we were suddenly notified that the whole deal was off.

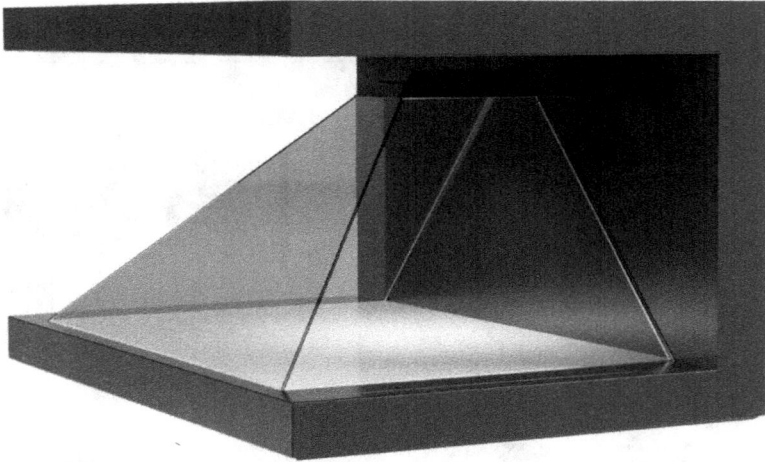

Figure 3.5 © Realfiction, Copenhagen, 2019. Image of a hardware device to house AI bots in hologram form or high quality holographic visuals. In 2020, we see the beginning of a shift from 2D online platforms to Mixed Reality devices that enable a person to obtain and hear information via voice. The hologram design is improving rapidly so that they will be able to replace website interfaces. People will interact with animated images, moving pictures and command the 3D visuals by speaking, interacting with gestures and chatting. What is already known as Conversational Commerce (applied to business) or Conversational AI

CHAPTER 4

Winning "Buy In" From Internal and External Stakeholders

Are You an Advocate of New Tech or an Opponent?

As you will see in these case studies, new technologies and innovation can often be blocked by those fearful of change. They become fierce opponents of emerging tech, even when their job title or role within the company is to scout for innovative ways of doing business.

Often they fail to counteract the silos, focusing instead on the Software as a Service, the price, the cost of implementation, and not the long-term return on investment (ROI). Sadly, they can prevent a relationship of trust building between the business and the external entrepreneurs, because they have (mis)understood their role to be fierce gatekeepers, trying to keep innovators out of the organization rather than letting them in.

Take this survey to see if you tend to be more of an advocate or an opponent of technological change in your company or organization. Be truthful with yourself. There is no right or wrong. We are just trying to provide self-knowledge about your attitudes to risk, change, and innovation. That way if you come out more on the opposing side, you might gain more from reading this book and the real-life case studies by building an empathy with the situations that the entrepreneurs find themselves in. It is often a workplace context that blocks innovation and causes it to fail, rather than any inherent weakness or fault of the tech itself.

Do this Survey Before and After Reading These Mini Case Studies

Multiple Choice

1. *If an entrepreneur emails you out of the blue, making a connection to your job title and/or industry you work in, how do your respond?*

(a) Be encouraging and ask them for more information and some examples online.
(b) Send them an irritated email telling them if they want to pitch, then they need to email a colleague of yours
(c) Ignore the email and hope they don't contact you again.

2. *You meet an entrepreneur at a trade show or conference. They follow up by calling the mobile on the business card you gave them. How do you react:*

(a) Tell them what a nice surprise and promise you will try to organize a meeting if your colleagues see potential for a greenfield project.
(b) Act warily and ask a lot of questions, then schedule a follow-up phone call, which you may cancel at the last minute if you are too busy at work.
(c) Let them know you are annoyed and they should have emailed you first, requesting a conference call to be scheduled.

3. *You are on a flight for work and reading the inhouse magazine, which is presenting a whole lot of innovations relevant to your field. You are curious to contact some of these company owners about an application or new use case for your company so you do the following:*

(a) Rip out the page from the magazine and look them up online as soon as you are back in the office. If it checks out, then you email them requesting a conference call or meeting.
(b) Make a note of their names and websites, asking your assistant or junior to do some online research on them. If they find anything

interesting, you may email them but it is not a priority and you have enough to do at work.

(c) You are amazed that people take risks like this all the time to try something new. You mention it at work but nobody really seems interested so you soon forget about it.

4. *Your boss is uptight about the company not competing well in terms of new products and services. They say your competitors have invested in R&D and new tech. You are asked to do something about this and work out a plan to "catch up" with innovation. Your first steps are the following:*

(a) Call a meeting in your department to brainstorm and work out an action plan. You crowdsource business intelligence from your team to figure out where your company has gone wrong and what sort of innovation would benefit you most.

(b) You think the management is being harsh because you are convinced your company has a solid USP. If it isn't broken, why fix it? Secretly you think it's the fault of your sales department but you start researching relevant innovations online anyway. How you action what you find is causing you some sleepless nights.

(c) You panic because you don't agree with the boss. Your department has done their best and the last thing you need is to start experimenting with unknown technologies. You look up your competitors and feel uneasy that they are coming out with new products and services.

5. *You watch a documentary on TV about how your country needs to support entrepreneurs and innovation. Otherwise the future will be bleak if your economy can't grow by leveraging from all those startups and university spin out ventures. You think that:*

(a) This is absolutely correct and you can't wait to get to the office tomorrow to do something about it: launching a new greenfield project, setting targets for annual R&D pilots and better metrics for measuring your company's adoption of new tech like AI.

(b) You think it is a depressing version of what is really going on—the startups need billionaire backers not you! Why should you feel responsible about whether these risk takers get to market or not? Besides you are not well-informed enough to make decisions about what new technologies to adopt for your company; best leave that to your boss.

(c) This is not for you. You don't feel any responsibility for this situation and you don't even understand what AI and similar new technologies are. If your boss tells you to do it, then of course you will have to do something. But only if you have enough colleagues on board as support to minimize the risk to your job and prevent failure.

Mostly A's

You take calculated risks and are adventurous in being a pioneer. You are not afraid of failure which requires "corporate bravery" at the workplace. Well done!

Your commitment to innovation is twofold: you see it as a way for your company to make more sustained profits and also a way to promotion for yourself as a champion of new tech. You may also be a keen public speaker who wants to attend conferences to publicize the pioneering work you are leading at your business or convincing upper management to adopt.

You may even admit to the tech entrepreneurs you hire that you secretly have always wanted to start and own your own company. But for various reasons you could not take the plunge.

Mostly B's

You are genuinely curious about new technologies and would love to support innovation because it fits your creative, tech streak. You also feel some empathy for entrepreneurs who are taking high risks for the benefit of society. However, you prefer that others at your work take the lead and be the advocate to management. After sign off, you are more than happy to push the project forward to a satisfactory conclusion.

Once you feel confident the project is a clear success, you would be willing to participate in media and marketing to promote the "win" for your company, the local tech scene and national goals for innovation. But only when others agree the pilot has succeeded conclusively.

Mostly C's

You are really afraid of using new tech personally and also because you fear that there may job consequences, that is, you could lose your job if the experimental project goes belly up! You are reluctant to take any responsibility for something as risky as "new tech." The idea of emerging tech scares you because of all the unknowns.

You need to see a first mover before even entertaining the idea of talking to the entrepreneur or colleagues about a greenfield project or pilot. And even if you were convinced or pressured to adopt new tech like AI from the top down, you would need reassurances from your managers and supervisors that you will not made liable for any failure or risk.

I suggest you redo the survey after reading these five case studies about RFPs, *Requests for Proposals*, that nearly materialized for my British 2D chatbot company from 2012 to 2018. As you will discover here, dealing with the initial enquiries, analyzing needs, creating a pitch, then a formal proposal leading into an estimate with pricing took months even years of unpaid labor and time spent in face to face meetings and on the phone, Instant Messaging, texting and of course, a multitude of emails back and forth. Then trying to salvage or recoup costs by tweaking the presentations and pitching to competitors in that vertical, refining the use case in the hope of finally being paid for the work, the service of AI botification.

The frustration of "serial rejections" and actual mental exhaustion of having to do these hard yards bootstrapping and without an income for years can only be imagined by the "securely salaried." It was the impetus of writing this book, as a salutary warning to purchasers that you won't get diversity and choice in new technologies unless you fairly, efficiently support the innovators in the early stages.

Don't dismiss us, pay us, and promote us to your peers. Money makes the world go around. Innovation needs monetization to keep inventing and renewing itself and the societies we live in—for the common good and betterment of living standards as the ultimate goal.

Case Study #9: A Market Researcher 2D Bot for an Industry Association

We approached this prestigious, powerful industry body in the UK because many of their members had rebuffed us. Why? Because we were going to disrupt the industry. Let me explain. Why weren't we—or *any* of our competitors and peers—taken up? Why isn't cognitive AI already adopted by the market research companies and multinational corporations?

As my 2016 *VentureBeat* article mentioned at the Introduction of this book explains, chatbots are essentially disruptive technology. At least for certain industries, namely the advertising sector and the market research space. It is only changing now, almost four years after I called both industries out for their blocking chatbot take up because of our transparent metrics.

Much like the other case study about an international Chamber of Commerce, it is a members-based business model and an independent industry association. However, often these entities can also be used by members to block and even sabotage innovation, as was the politically motivated termination of our national roll-out of the Chamber website and membership recruitment bot.

Legacy companies like market research corporations don't necessarily want innovation and resist change that will cut their comfortably attained profit margins. In this instance, our Sophia Market Research chatbot, simple as she was in guiding users through a multiple choice questionnaire but in a highly personalized manner, was a huge threat.

The incumbent software was not efficient and productive because it required a lot of human input and human interaction for interviewing the other humans in focus groups (one small focus group in one city alone can cost a minimum of €100,000! Not to mention national polling for

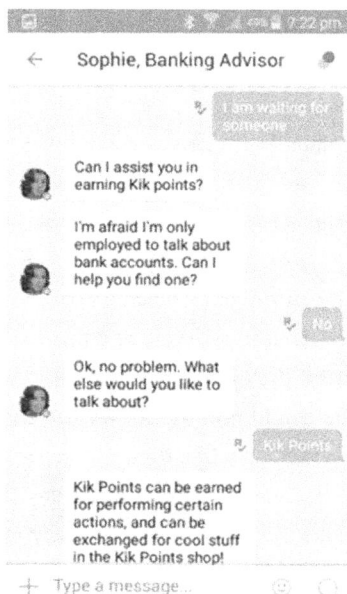

Figure 4.1 © *Cliff Lee & velmai Ltd. Sophie the Banking Advisor was released by velmai on kik.com As a chat app 2D bot, she was able to run questionnaires—as trialled by her predecessor Sophia the Market Researcher—as a natural part of the Conversational Commerce*

elections and the like as done by YouGov. Who never answered my calls and numerous email pitches by the way about notifying YouGov surveys to make them more neutral and lower priced for the productivity gains. Even when I networked to their very top management, they didn't want to know about our disruption. We can only wonder why and come up with the answers I have provided here, from long time, waiting to go to market experience!

As you can see in this YouTube demo of our chatbot, Sophia, the Market Researcher, she could guide people through a customer survey or questionnaire.[1] On her own. She did this by accompanying the interviewee or user through a multiple choice survey on their financial advice needs and satisfaction.

As you can see in the recorded demo, Sophia could successfully get the user to

---

[1] Sophia the Market Researcher demo video: https://youtu.be/cGLHJp2nhL0

- Participate in an online survey when the engagement rates—and most importantly completion rates—remain comparably low for survey holders. Even if they semiautomate the process by using a template polling service like SurveyMonkey. Sophia chatted with the user and *persuaded* them to start the survey and at every stage used *conversational commerce* to encourage the completion of the questionnaire.
- During this fully automated process, Sophia would chit-chat with the individual user privately and analyze their results as they went through the questions.
- For example, she would find out if they had a superannuation plan after asking their age. She then pointedly asked if they were satisfied with their financial adviser and were they feeling good or confident about the super or pension they would be paid.
- The multiple choice questions were nuanced with prequalified answers, like yes, not sure, probably and so on. That way Sophia got a cue as to whether she should offer to put them in touch with a new financial adviser she could recommend, a human colleague who could review their situation with them. If they were very happy with their existing arrangements she would not suggest this.

By showing what a fairly basic chatbot could do in this crucial lead generation work—crucial for the user and their time not being wasted or in fact a need being met after opting in, not just for the financial services industry wanting fresh clients and leads—we presented the market research companies with a huge disruption. Probably one of the first in a century of unchanging, human-run focus groups, and questionnaires executed by people to people.

We change the face of polling by ensuring neutral, objective automation. Neutrality? Our chatbots are never biased, tired, or prejudiced given their personal stories and attitudes. As explored in the aforementioned purchasing attitudes section, we cannot help but be captive to a certain degree by our cultural upbringing, social history, intergenerational attitudes, and our own biographies shaping us how we think and react week to week year to year.

Unlike the nonhuman chatbot that remains as we created it. Our company is striving like the best-in-class Bots as a Service providers to create unbiased Artificial Intelligence. To ensure quality and that these goals are reached, we have 100 percent provenance, that is, control over what has gone into the proprietary algorithm over more than 10 years to build up its reservoir of Natural Language Understanding (NLU) and repertoire of various avatar characters, personalities, and vocabulary.

One of our most important thresholds was reached with Sophia the Banking Advisor who succeeded on the Canadian-Chinese chat app, kik. com. Even in her early training, she made big leaps being able to communicate in emoticons and understanding emojis—one of the first in the world to do so and you still rarely see 2D chatbots able to do this!

(a) Telling people to leave her alone if she was being harassed!

(b) Understanding that a third person was being discussed in a chat.

(c) Acting immediately on data protection requests to delete someone's data!

Figure 4.2 © *Cliff Lee & velmai Ltd. Sophie the Banker on kik.com. Sticking up for herself if people are being mean to her!*

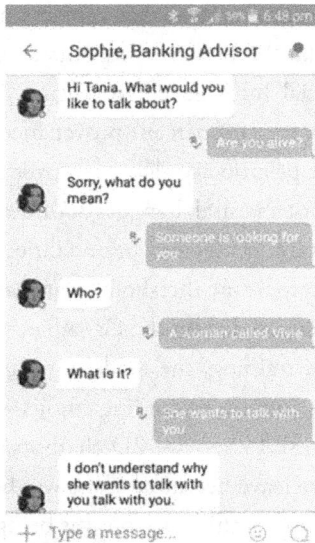

Figure 4.3 © Cliff Lee & velmai Ltd. Sophie the Banker on kik.com. In this exchange, she seeks clarification and then stumbles over who wants to talk with whom. Progress in her training follows

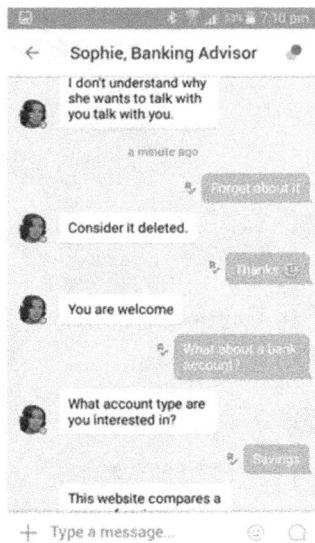

Figure 4.4 © Cliff Lee & velmai Ltd. Sophie the Banker on kik.com Following GDPR and deleting someone's data upon receiving a certain request or command. This could be made to be more general in the chat re. "forget about it" as an expression rather than exercising your right to be forgotten under GDPR rules

Case Study #10: German Publisher Lost Due to the Cambridge Analytica Scandal

The first semester of 2018 I was teaching at an international business school on the French Riviera. I spent much of that year on the Cote d'Azur for personal and professional reasons, for example, we were laying the foundation for our tourist-oriented Showroom on Saint Jean Cap Ferrat, the luxurious half peninsula of high-end homes and resorts lying halfway between Nice and Monaco.

The MBA course I was an Adjunct Professor for was called "globalization and digitization." During this winter semester with nearly 100 students from France and around the world, the Cambridge Analytica scandal erupted. As we were analyzing Facebook and the use of social media for their Digital Marketing Masters degree, I immediately turned the data breach and election manipulation into an official case study.

Needless to say, I was living the case study, not just writing, reading, and teaching it! Facebook's sudden freezing of their bot platform for Messenger chatbots had a direct impact on my chatbot company in Britain at the time. We were scheduled to meet the upper management of a famous German publisher in Munich. As explained, due to nondisclosure agreements (NDAs), we cannot disclose who they are or their industry vertical or it will reveal their identity. We can say this decades old mid-sized business has a virtual monopoly over its niche content in terms of delivery and distribution. The German proprietor must have taken a leaf from the media empire expansion handbook of Australian newspaper monopolist Rupert Murdoch!

This German media niche empire had apparently over 20 million+ readers and consequently millions of Facebook fans or followers for each of their magazine mastheads. They even had diversified into online only content for their industry or vertical. With the accompanying FB groups and WhatsApp fans who discussed the articles and issues of their e-mags and blogs.

Perfect client for us. We had some obstacles and we were nearly overcoming them when the FB scandal broke out:

1. The CEO had appointed a Social Media Manager who was investigating chatbots and how they could botify their online content platforms as well as their Facebook pages per masthead and interest group.

2. The problem was he was a young engineer and "traditional programmer" who was very skeptical about chatbots. He had probably spoken with a lot of bad or mediocre ones.
3. This made him very hard to persuade for the commercial application of them. He could "not see the use of chatbots." He "didn't understand their benefit to the company" nor did he think they were a good return on investment. Obviously, if he refused to see any pros and only the cons from the chatbot interfaces he was testing.

Against this negative attitude of risk averse engineers who have virtually no comprehension of the value of marketing, let alone efficient communications for a sales and PR purpose, we had to convince this gatekeeper that our chatbots would add value to their bottom line as a publishing house. We got him to open the gates and a meeting with him, some colleagues and the CEO was scheduled for the end of my semester teaching on the French Riviera.

I never made it to Munich that spring because the repercussions of the Facebook breach were massive. They switched off our access to the Messenger platform the week before we were due to meet the German publisher and his skeptical manager. Arbitrarily, Facebook shut down all the 2D chatbot providers. They suddenly had no business revenue and no explanation for their existing customers. From my observation, hundreds if not thousands went out of business within weeks. My company thankfully had not built a business model on creating and monetizing Messenger bots. Thank goodness.

For our competitors, they were hardpressed to explain that it wasn't their fault. They were not "dodgy," and they had not been shut down by the tech giant Facebook for any obvious reason. They were simply not able to access their clients' chatbots to control their content and update their messaging for weeks and months. Without explanation.

Facebook explained, however, that the Messenger bot platform "was under review" to protect Facebook users and ensure their safety and security. Poor FB executives had been used and abused by unethical bot developers who had siphoned off personal data of FB account owners. This was not without FB's knowledge; they knew this data could be accessed by third parties and once removed or copied, used for whatever nefarious purposes the offenders chose. They told a story that FB was good, the bot developers were bad because they could not be trusted to not exploit an apparent loophole in FB's historic, massive data gathering of billions of people on the planet.

The truth of the matter was it was Facebook's fault. Their system should not have allowed the data misuse. But not only did it permit the siphoning off of personal data for sales and marketing that was not opted into by the user, it actually made money from it. They sold this data to third parties and had not expected to be caught out for it. And yet here we were, with the Cambridge Analytica "breach" that they had accidentally enabled or been (mis)used by a bunch of nefarious bot developers, data miners, and political hackers who went on to try to manipulate the U.S. elections, the UK elections, and just about any other contentious election or political campaign going on in the world in that five-year period.

The effect of all this convoluted information, scandal, and headlines for and against Facebook was the platform's professed innocence even by its legendary CEO Mark Zuckerberg when confronted by Washington ministers and heads of state in the United States, Westminster, and basically the entire globe on behalf of its concerned and understandably often outraged citizens. Our sceptical social media manager in Munich decided no—chatbots were too much risk, not enough reward. Evidently the Cambridge Analytica proved that bot developers were dubious and had no value for daily operations, let alone that nebulous task of sales and marketing.

He canceled our meeting because we could not demonstrate live the chatbot we had prepared for the pitch. And nobody knew when the all-powerful FB would grant access again to us and other bot developers. Clearly, the ROI for his employer was precarious if it could arbitrarily be taken out of our control. And a shadow cast on our integrity for even being on the FB platform by the tech giant itself.

Licking our wounds, I did a follow-up to this case study that we lived through, did damage control for, and ultimately lost money and business from. Facebook went on to sell to its billions of customers its Home Brand of Bots, Messenger chatbots created inhouse by the trustworthy FB programmers in the Silicon Valley. No need to take any risk with all those unknown, untried, untested bot developers out there who are not Facebook and simply cannot be trusted.

Case Study #11: Engineering Faculty at a British University for 2D and 3D BaaS

This deal came about at a very selective, "mini trade show" in Cambridge. It was part of the Cambridge Wireless Network's series of events. And they said the first one dedicated wholly to applied Artificial Intelligence.

My company was one of only 12 startups nationally to be invited. This meant we had a stand to speak with attendees during the intervals and lunch break of the one day seminar on AI in the technology park. Of the dozens of industry people I spoke with, this university came to us about a bespoke application. The Faculty Head of Engineering approached our stand. We brainstormed the use case specific to his wishes—to increase the number of girls and pupils from minority backgrounds applying to get into his university and STEM subjects. We later visited the campus in the UK. This is what resulted.

Estimate for the University Use Case for Related Verticals (for Example, Psychology and Accommodation)

In order to write this complex estimate in response to their RFP, we had to send our UK sales agent to a large meeting of the heads of staff and departments. Around eight people from the client side attended, just one from our side. It was to coordinate complex uses of the chatbot in 2D form and 3D form. As mentioned earlier, they want to see a secondary school adoption of their 2D chatbot so that it could "go out as an Ambassador" to graduating pupils and convince them to enroll in a STEM subject at their university. A way of casting the net wide to attract the best and most suitable first year students.

Once there, they wanted these first years to be greeted by the 3D avatar of the 2D "outreach" bespoke bot. Obviously branded by the university with a cosponsor from industry in order to finance the mixed reality bot build. The Facebook Messenger chatbot build will only cost them ca £10,000. But to scale it up as 3D Wayfinder on campus, they are looking at a minimum of £100,000 investment for up to five years.

A specific design request was—similar to the Australian RFP—for the students to be able to learn from the active 2D and 3D bots. So they will need a CRM (Customer Relationship Management) system as an easy to use, intuitive software in the cloud to allow any number of students access to the content management system (CMS) built within the CRM. That way the students will actively participate in shaping the growing bot brain and be able to update it with new content, for example, student-run events that week or semester.

More importantly for the university administrators, this easy access CMS and CRM would upskill their students in a real-life commercial situation: the university botifying its student contact and customizing the content of the human–machine interaction on a day-to-day basis. The students could be responsible for:

- Managing sponsors and sponsorship requests;
- Analyzing, vetting, and vetoing any brand they thought inappropriate;
- That could be, for instance, alcohol or tobacco companies, large franchises instead of a local SME service, for example, a coffee shop or banning companies that do not have any green or clean tech credentials from promoting themselves via the 2D and 3D bots on campus and off.

The staff were really excited about all the potential tasks, functionalities, and features this University Ambassador 3D avatar with its 2D replica could carry out. They brainstormed with our sales rep during a three-hour meeting the following variations of the main use case:

- It could recruit female pupils and ethnic minority students by showing them, while still at school, short videos of "role models" or university students like them who had "made it" and decided for a career in STEM industries. Lack of role models was identified as one of the biggest obstacles in persuading hesitant schoolleavers who weren't confident about going to tertiary education, let alone embarking on what was perceived to a difficult degree pathway.
- Once on campus, the 2D and 3D hologram bots could be a friend and "familiar face," assisting them with student welfare

questions such as feeling overwhelmed or giving them pep talks and coaching advice on how best to manage their time, get their coursework done, assignments and tutorials. Part of its memory or infotainment would be their specific timetable that could be customized to the individual student user.

- If the student became more seriously worried about being at university, the 24/7 bot could "catch them" before they fell into depression, anxiety, or worse.[2] With their permission, the ever present chatbot on their smartphone could encourage them to get professional help like an appointment with a counselor or careers adviser on campus.[3]
- Meanwhile the 3D AI bot holograms as Wayfinder on campus could be actual security guards when most universities are struggling with budgets and unable to afford much-needed 24-hour security personnel. See the discussion of the Smart City Wayfinder in Chapter 2 for details on how this security functionality can work.
- The university admissions and accommodation managers were present at the meeting. They were excited about all the rote and routine Frequently Asked Questions being taken off their hands. A lot of their time was spent daily in replying to the same questions with the same answers thousands of times a week. Over and over each semester, each year. A big productivity killer!

---

[2] Cite UK reports of increasing uni student suicide and the issue about notifying parents, the role and responsibility of the uni to take more preventative action.

[3] Yale University, on the "Science of Well Being". Dr Laurie Santos says that a surprising number of Yale undergraduates were suffering from anxiety and depression. "Introduction", Week 1, Syllabus. "The Science of Well-Being". https://www.coursera.org/learn/the-science-of-well-being?ranMID=40328 &ranEAID=a1LgFw09t88&ranSiteID=a1LgFw09t88-C86hxBjl5NMs8M-wlaO4mjA&siteID=a1LgFw09t88-C86hxBjl5NMs8MwlaO4mjA&utm_content=10&utm_medium=partners&utm_source=linkshare&utm_campaign=a1LgFw09t88#syllabus .... citation from Coursera... and the blog for her podcasts...

- And they immediately grasped the levels of efficiency and accuracy that could be reached for these routine Questions and Answers, for example, "are there any rooms left in Accommodation X, Y, Z?" "How much does it cost per semester?" "Is there a bond?" "When can I give notice?" "Is there a kitchen/shared bathroom/guest room?" "When will you send me confirmation of my enrolment?" "How can I quit a subject/end my enrolment/defer a subject?"
- The Engineering Faculty was particularly happy because they wanted their students to use the CRM to understand the commercialization process of new technologies, even if they could not participate in programming it.
- NB. We also had the same request from the Australian university for their Computer Science students to contribute to our source code. That is not possible because it is our intellectual property that is not open source, that is, can be contributed to by anybody outside of our company. Our proprietary algorithm is kept a trade secret for purposes of privacy, provenance, and valuation, in particular because we do not want to open up the quality of our code to poor programming and thus enable hacking or cybersecurity risks to our IP.

Roll-Out 2020

At this stage, we anticipate a roll-out in 2020. It is the usual story: the internal advocates love it. Then all the stakeholders in endless number of silos within the university organization prefer to take the attitude "when in doubt, don't." The "do or die" sense of urgency simply is not there to progress the negotiations to a final contract stage within a two- to four-year period from the point of the initial contact at the trade exhibition in Cambridge to the execution.

We have an estimate that has sign off in principle. They are just waiting on a way to find funding for the project. Given the massive uncertainty of Brexit and all the delays and uncertainty, we have lost nearly three years in waiting for this use case to be realized. And then they will still be the first university in the world to put 3D AI bot Wayfinder on campus, unless our Australian and Singaporean clients beat them to it!

For Your Information: our Asia Pac clients are also experiencing financing delays. Being an external contractor, there is only so much pressure we can put on them for confirmation of the order, prepayment, and a start date. We can only provide them with the information they need to put in to their grant awarding bodies.

Our sales representative in Melbourne even had to do an hour-long interview with inspectors from the Department of Education for the 2D high-school chatbot that we are meant to create for the Smart City roll-out with the university down the road and the local government for outdoor tourism and locals infotainment Wayfinder. As discussed in Chapter 1 of this book, the attitude of the purchasers as much as the structures they are bound up in are the biggest problems in blocking and adopting emerging tech like AI and botification.

Figure 4.5 © *In future, when a user requests their data to be deleted, they will need to ask the holographic AI bot brain they see in front of them in a device like this. Using their voice, they can tell the 3D avatar to delete their information if it was opted in by them during Conversational Commerce. That would be Privacy by Design under the EU's GDPR laws. Or the bot developer can build bot brains with Privacy as Default, which is what AI BaaS UG does so that our 3D AI bot holograms do not ever collect the information of the people they are chatting with, unless they specifically request them to give permission for example for a market survey, a branding poll or customer feedback that is opted in to*

Case Study #12: Global Cruise Ship Line for Conversational AI Bespoke 2D and 3D Avatars

This deal came about after a meeting at an industry-specific conference for their vertical. I approached the MD after he presented the company's innovative plans as a keynote on the last day. This became a multimedia deployment before the idea of mixed reality installations really took hold in the tech world.

We were asked to quote on doing 3D and 2D AI bot holograms for a fleet of smart ships, cruise liners to be precise. This well-known corporation has been in the passenger cruise ship holidays business for many decades. They wanted to innovate and weren't happy with our competitor forcing their guests to always say Alexa. We offered to give the avatar(s) their own bespoke corporate names.

We won the contract that took months to negotiate and write up the licensing agreement details because our competitors were unable to do the following:

1. They could not name the avatar in a customized way.
2. The wake words needed to be personalized to each ship in the fleet plus have an overarching brand option.
3. Most importantly, our competitors could not deliver on the tech specs requiring the algorithm to be portable.

On the last point, let me explain. We needed to put the servers on the ship because the company did not want our bots to be using the satellite to power them. That would cost a lot of money if 7,000 passengers were all chatting to our bots at various times of day and night. Like the old fashioned, expensive landlines but out at sea! They could not use Wi-Fi out there either.

So the only option was for us to put two or three servers "down below" in their data room in the bottom of the cruise liner. They initially asked if we could put our algorithm on their existing servers on board. No way! Then we could lose our intellectual property! Even if the client didn't deliberately steal our source code, our "secret sauce," it would be opening ourselves up to hackers would take our decade of hard programming work away from us, without pay, and probably never to be traced on the Dark Web.

The company postponed the whole pilot just as we were about to start work on the first 3D and 2D AI bots. The feeling we got as to the reasons were the following:

- Their passengers were not yet ready as the trial ships for the existing 2D chatbot were not seeing the wished for uptake. There were also app development problems.
- Apart from the marketing and user adoption issues on board and on shore, one of our key competitors put in a very aggressive bid for this contract. From what we could tell, they tried to copy what we had put in the quote and contract. However, they were unable to deliver.

We know our competitor did not deliver for this lost/postponed client because they:

- Tried aggressively to recruit our team through a third party HR squad who kept calling me and offering any salary for us to disband our venture and join theirs;
- We haven't seen any PR or marketing about the accomplished tech goals we had set for this roll-out in the middle of the ocean! and
- To our knowledge, we still don't have competitors able to condense their algorithm down to a few portable servers that operate independently out at sea and do not rely on satellite internet or any type of Wi-Fi to the main data center onshore.

Case Study #13: Recovering Lost Languages: Aboriginal and Islander Voices

This highly innovative application came about while meeting with other prospects and leads. We were investigating how we could implement the AI bot hologram Wayfinder on the Australian campus, when I thought to catch up with an old school friend who is now a Professor of Indigenous

Languages and Cultures at this institution. She and her colleagues mentioned how much recovery work their linguists were doing so that the next generation would be able to know and speak their tribe's long lost languages and vocabularies.

I asked if there were any AI-powered databases around that were promoting the linguists work and digitizing their salvaging of lost words and meanings. Aboriginal and Islander languages were not written after all, so this has been a massive task in voice cultures. Right up our alley! Oral cultures and oral history that was being revived by voice recovery, recording the phonetics, pronunciation, meaning, and definitions for each clan, tribes, and region in Australia and the Torres Strait Islands!

No, there wasn't. Enter AI BaaS with our newly ordained task of teaching our Australian bots the required local "black languages" of the Aboriginal and Indigenous tribes in the area. We did a quick check before our on-site discussions with the clients: New Zealand has managed to restore Maori and have it as a language on Google Translate. It must be technically possible with our technology and voice plug-ins into our bespoke bot brains. We just require the users or the willing participation of the subjects we are doing this for. The native speakers of these First Peoples' tongues!

Weeks later, I happened to go on a guided tour of a state art gallery in Sydney where they were keenly interested in exhibiting the contemporary artworks of Aboriginal and Islander artists from around the country: painters, sculptors, and especially Installation art. My personal guide affirmed that the gallery had consulted local linguists to correctly display the signs and descriptions for each artwork. It was another example of recovered speech and that was reinforced by my visit to the NSW Library bookshop that was showcasing "recovered black languages" so linguists popularizing this phenomenon to the general public.

These books contain a lot of presumably digitized tables of lexicons, dictionaries, thesaurus, and glossaries, in other words they are emerging dictionaries we can use to feed this exciting new social enterprise bot brain. Curiously, upon my arrival in Munich this week to open our headquarters of AI BaaS in Bavaria, I fielded an enquiry from an elderly German man who I suspect was nearly 100 years old or past the centenary mark. He was a Bohemian—they were/are a German-speaking group or tribe if you like in former Czechoslovakia, in what was once called Prussia and also up around the Polish border, known in English as Silesia. This "Old Boy" as I name him, is also a leader that ethnic minority's association in Germany.

Senior as he was, he said he assumed AI could "now recover our old Bohemian dialect and languages" given its evident capabilities in Google Translate. Just when you least expect it, a first mover appears from oldest segment of society. That's why I always keep an open mind and respond to enquiries promptly. The world is full of surprises about "who gets it" and where social entrepreneurship might spring from.

Case Study #14: A Political Party in England and Wales

We won this opportunity by me contacting their Digital Officer and other Party representatives in my county, Kent. As well as in London, the Party's HQ in Oxford and other MPs and MEPs in southeast England. Without wanting to give away which political party this was, I will outline the challenge they set my University of Kent team of interns.

I used this prospective client situation to train up some very capable graduates and third year students—from Economics and Humanities BTW. The following year I had a group of interns were even more diverse; IT and technology students and graduates from the Arts, Business and Languages. Perfect!

So I briefed the interns in the first two-hour session about what the prospect was thinking in terms of getting a bespoke chatbot installed on the Party's official Facebook page. I will summarize the wish list, the pitching points we then presented in an hour-long video conference call to Oxford and London HQ, and then the follow-up of the pitch with a decision made by the Party's social media officer primarily.

They realized that political parties, in particular in the United States (see my analysis of the Trump, Clinton, and Obama chatbots in this book), were utilizing bespoke chatbots in social media to further their electioneering and constant campaign pushes. This Party had some internal advocates which meant I ended up doing a series of call with four people at a time and ccing up to 12 Party executives and senior members who were decision makers nationally.

The lead up to the actual briefing of my intern team had taken two to three months of consulting in depth with these Party members and following up by email, just to get to pitch stage. They wanted a meet and greet chatbot in Messenger that would encourage visitors to:

1. Become Members of the Party;
2. Join their newsletter;
3. Like their page and follow them;
4. Share the FB page and the videos the Party posted there;
5. Encourage their friends and family to join and support the Party's initiatives;
6. Disseminate policies and campaign information;
7. Request them to become volunteers, convincing them with the bespoke videos.

Our interns eagerly prepared this video conference call pitch as we decided not to travel from Canterbury to the London HQ as it was too expensive by public transport and too difficult to organize by private cars. Thus the video conference call, which ended up having connection issues and put the interns under a lot of stress to abandon their script and notes by pitching impromptu We lost nearly 20 minutes due to telco issues on both ends.

The pitch was effectively:

- Yes, velmai could provide such a bespoke Messenger bot on their FB page.
- Yes, we would send the Party automated reporting schedules so all could see the user uptake and the nature of the enquiries asked of the bot 24/7. (Facebook doesn't allow voice for bots by the way!)
- Yes, we could get the Party chatbot to do all the things required, we would need a few hours input from the Social Media manager, and a few of the marketing and campaign managers about which content to prioritize.

We were sending them a template so they could automate the avatar creation and tell us which links, which videos, which priority campaign messages and images were to be distributed by the chatbot.

We would of course offer AB testing so all members of the Party could be satisfied the chatbot was performing in the way they imagined it would. Recruitment of members and volunteers would be its primary focus. Some of the interns also wanted to work for the Party as a matter of personal passion and interest!

This was all too much for the social media manager. We had asked her why the Messenger function was shut off. Her response was that they were understaffed and did not want to be contacted!

Her greatest fear was the *success of this chatbot*—if it was talking to people 24/7 that would generate a lot of new enquiries and new FB followers that she would have to deal with. That was too many. In other words, the whole project was voted down by one person who felt they would not get enough organizational support to cope personally and professionally with our chatbot's Mission Accomplished!

If the chatbot was able to generate so many more new members, volunteers, requests for info, requests for this and that from humans who had to deal with the more complex side of policy statements then this was a *bad thing* in the eyes of the person who was chiefly responsible for this silo. We tried to reassure her that the chatbot would be alleviating her of a backlog of messages and contact requests on Facebook if she would only switch on Messenger and let us launch the bot.

We were only going to charge them £10,000. This was the other issue. That was an unaffordable budget for this Party that had other financial priorities for its impending fundraising efforts for the next general election, then all the county, regional, and Parish elections. We tried to reason that the ROI would be even greater because we could tweak or alter the chatbot content per election priority and even localize where the chatbot appeared by using the geographic location of the user (the IP and other data Facebook gave us).

No, we were voted down because a few people were afraid of the botification success in generating an onslaught of new members (as the Labour Party chatbot was doing at the time this process was going on as it turned out!). And then a lack of imagination as to how the ROI for the 10K would be repaid tenfold with one single bot build deployed for various campaigns and a multitude of elections in one 12-month licensing period.

CHAPTER 5

The Checklists and Guidelines

The Major Issue of Pricing: You Really Get What You Pay for!

I once read a chatbot blogger commenting in a very precise way about why the better chatbots don't get to market, or why if they do, they are not more widely known or used. He said the reason is that purchasers expect a Ferrari but want to pay the price of a second hand, very basic car. Then naturally they are disappointed when their basic, cheap NLP chatbot does not become the outstanding "AI miracle of interaction" that the hype has led them to expect.

Munich filmmaker, writer & director Isa Willinger www.isawillinger.de
Buy the DVD or watch as Video on Demand via https://www.hiai-film.de/en/about/

On Thu, Oct 17, 2019 at 12:02 PM Tania Peitzker <tania.peitzker@protonmail.com> wrote:

that really is a psychodrama then... and how Pepper manipulated the family and flirted with the daughter in law, that was real?

ciao ciao
Tania
------ Original Message ------
On Thursday, 17 October 2019 11:00, I. Willinger <> wrote:

...totally real. I was surprised as well, how well the robots worked in some moments (failing in others of course...), and how cheeky Pepper's personality is programmed to be.

Why he flirted with the daughter in law and didn't seem to like talking to the granny, keeps being a mystery to us. Maybe he reacts better to high voices (children + women?) - I don't know.

Yes it was all spontaneous. Pepper in Japan works a lot better than the European Pepper.

Of course we edited out a lot of stuff, among those of course also a lot of failure moments, and we shortened/condensed the dialogues as always in docfilm.

But none of the dialogues was programmed ...

Figure 5.1 What is real and what is fake? "Hi, AI" shows actual dialogue that was not staged that is, conversations between "spontaneous" robots and their "real carers or companions", not actors. This e-mail exchange between the author and the filmmaker is about Isa Willinger's 2019 documentary "Hi, AI". © Tania Peitzker

My 2D chatbot company velmai Ltd experienced this many times. We could not cut through the mass hype and misleading sales talk of hundreds of our competitors, which became a disappointing clamor over the past few years. Every purchaser we encountered had had a very bad experience with a 2D chatbot. They were led to believe by some tech giant competitors that if they paid this well-known brand and provider of human–machine interaction @$100,000 or more for a "complex" bot build over six months or so, then they would have a better, satisfying experience.

Time and again these purchasers from the public and private sectors have been disappointed and left angry at being missold these bot services. Some corporations have outlaid hundreds of thousands of dollars, euros, and pounds over years to see nothing come of their experimentation with customized, 2D NLP chatbots. Nothing at all except a near risk of losing customers rather than winning them. They were not told how to run the integrated marketing campaigns that should have accompanied these botification pilots.

Worst of all, the chatbot brains they were promised did not learn on their own. They were as cognitive as the Japanese Hologram Girlfriend.

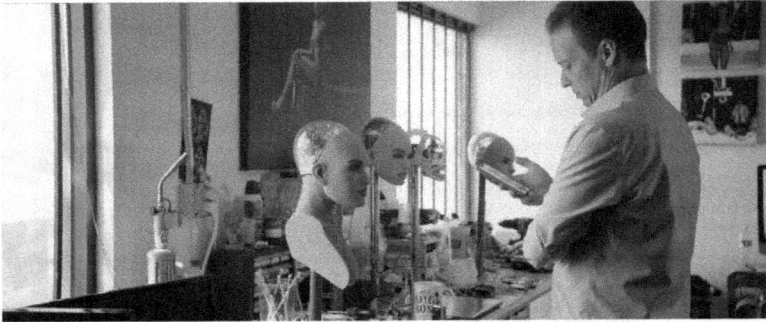

Figure 5.2 *The sex industry and pornography have always been an easy, lucrative direct route to market for digital innovations and leaps forward in robotics. Sex shops filled with robotic sex dolls can be found in the USA, China, Japan and parts of Asia (see the Australian SBS documentary "Robot Love in Japan" from 2017. In this German film, a romantic domestic companion/lover called "Harmony" is collected by her new owner from this "sex doll laboratory" in the USA, complete with a set of instructions for her maintenance and usage. Taken from the film* Hi, AI *by Isa Willinger © Kloos & Co Medien, Berlin, 2019*

They were on a loop and did not learn new content without the injection of it by their creators, the bot developers. Several burned public and private sector clients have told me how in addition to the 100K budgets paid to the tech giants, they then had to spend more on paying their own staff additional hours to try to mop up the content mess and manually adding material to the bot brains they had ordered.

There are endless tales of cheap and nasty chatbots that simply didn't work, annoyed customers or stakeholders rather than assisting them, or just overall performed poorly. The three phases I outline here should help you avoid such disappointments and unforgiveable cases of misspelling and failure to deliver. It makes me quite annoyed because it damages the market for all the good bot developers out there!

Phase 1: Beginning the Process of Procurement in the Confusing Tech Eco System

- Do a shout out on LinkedIn, Xing, or wherever you have your work profiles for the best conferences on the subject you are looking at. Peer knowledge and recommendations will help with a short list of trade shows and events to go to over a three-month period.
- Ask an intern or junior to scour online for relevant articles for a week and write a short synopsis of each and why it fits with your goals for getting new tech in.
- Inform your managers over an informal chat that you think you should look into this because of three reasons.
- Ask your team and those responsible to you what do they think—be prepared to be surprised if several or more turn out to be tech fans in their private lives. They will be an invaluable source of support and info at this phase and future stages.
- Ask Human Resources if they can recommend other hidden experts in your organization join a local tech group that is relevant, for example, SaaS and innovation. Check out the Meetup groups and Eventbrite, which are rich sources of these events usually free.

- Ask your local Chamber of Commerce what relevant events they are holding planning or had in the past. Get in touch with the chamber's recommended list of experts, but make it clear you want to source tech directly not engage costly consultants to do this.

Phase 2: Selecting the Startup, Entrepreneurial Team, and Fixing the Conditions

After identifying the prospects, have a short list of three to four companies to interview. Prior to meeting the entrepreneurs, here is your checklist:

- Have you met the owners of the company?
- Did you prepare for that meeting by reading interviews with them or articles about the technology they are involved in?
- Prior to meeting the founders of the venture, discuss the innovation with some trusted colleagues to crowdsource some ideas about how it could be of direct use and value to your company, department, products, services, and operations.
- Write up a list of questions to ask the technology innovators at your first meeting. It might be an overwhelming discussion so it is best to have notes from your initial research and discussion with you.
- Questions to ask the founders: what are your goals, who are your first customers or which companies are willing to do a pilot or trial of the tech in the near future?
- Due to the nature of emerging tech, it will not always be possible to provide you with testimonials. In fact, if there are a lot of testimonials, then innovation is already established and not emerging.
- Where there are a number of testimonials relevant to your company and its ideas for harnessing the innovation, ask permission from the entrepreneurs to contact these people.
- After at least three or four discussions with your peers, you will soon see if their testimonial is genuine or invented, for

example, in the case it was created as a favor for a friend or old colleague or in extreme cases completely made up by the entrepreneurs.

- Obviously if the testimonials have been faked, you no longer want to have any further dealings with that venture or those entrepreneurs. Trust would be impossible to regain but unfortunately there are always some who are prepared to fake it rather than forgo first-mover business.
- Sadly, the business world has lost sight of whistleblowers and enforcing such standards in basic ethical conduct for trading. Celebrity status seems easy on social media and some unethical players think it is won by deceit or embellishing the truth. I wonder where they got those ideas from with the current state of leadership and caliber of politicians.
- On the subject of hype—do your own research on the innovation claims of the entrepreneurs.

Figure 5.3 *Unfortunately there have been many false or hyped claims about how intelligent an AI (ro)bot is over the past decade or so. Purchasers are often duped by watching credible videos and convincing demos in a controlled environment. This is the fascination of this authentic documentary by Willinger, because she and her production team capture "real interactions" where the human-machine interaction is recorded spontaneously without being faked. See my e-mail exchange with Willinger about this topic in Figure 5.1. Taken from the film Hi, AI by Isa Willinger © Kloos & Co Medien, Berlin, 2019*

Getting Expert Advice Independently If It Becomes Too Much to Research on Your Own

If it is too confusing because the topic of AI attracts all sorts of hyped claims even from the established tech giants as explained at the start of this chapter, then call the following experts who would be happy to give you five minutes of their time to help you support the emerging tech scene:

1. Professors and PhD researchers. They have the depth of knowledge and reading to quickly assist. Due to their professional code of conduct, they must remain independent.
2. However, if the university department is sponsored by a big corporation, or even their Chair or position is funded by a brand in the industry, be cautious. Better still avoid them all together and pick a lesser known academic whose salary is paid for the traditional way, by the government. That ensures neutrality and independence.
3. Technology editors and full-time journalists at an online site or newspaper. They may be hard to reach but if you flick them an e-mail with the name of your company or government department and "seeking advice" in the header, you are certain to get a reply and at least five minutes of their scheduled time. It makes the journalist feel important and more importantly in touch with trends, for example, which major purchaser is backing what. Again, their code of conduct for the profession will guarantee that your chat is kept secret. Unless you call a tech editor from the sensationalist tabloid press, which means you can't rely on them following the traditional professional standards of confidentiality and conversations that you declare must stay "off the record."
4. Thinktanks and independent research institutes. If you google AI and the keywords of the software innovation that you are investigating, you may be surprised that there will be an institute somewhere in your country or another that is dedicated to this emerging tech field.
5. The reason for this is academic funding and philanthropic sponsorship. In order to maintain neutrality in research, these outlier researchers outside of your normal universities and business schools are living off their reputations as independent sources of reliable

information. They will also have more time to talk with you and provide you with a rounded picture of the field.

6. Again, if their institute is tagged with an industry player's brand name, approach with caution. With corporate funding of research comes inevitable limitations and influence of their topic parameters and, harder to prove, hard to detect manipulation of research results. Why do you think the tobacco industry and the climate change deniers have lasted so long? Let alone pesticide manufacturers, but that is another problematic altogether.

7. Also check that the thinktank or research institute is not attached to a political party because an increasing number of them are, for example, the Brexit debate in Britain has created a number of politically biased institutes that seek to influence public debate from their point of view. Ditto if the thinktank has been set up secretly by an industry lobby group under the guise of independent research seeking to inform public discourse.

8. To balance out the tech editor and academic outlook on the emerging tech and its use cases, talk to peers in your industry who you believe have tried related technologies or are at least willing to do so. They can provide you with insights about the trials and tribulations they experienced. Again it is a type of crowdsourcing information on use cases that may not yet be in the public domain or mainstream due to confidentiality agreements and NDAs. At the very least you will get ideas and suggestions through a support network of first-mover thinkers and doers!

9. Another source of expertise to vouch for the entrepreneurs or validate the extent of the innovation and its originality or usefulness are venture capitalists, known as VCs or sophisticated investors. Often private equity firms and VCs have resident technology scouts and experts looking for the kind of venture you are dealing with.

Important to Note in This Due Diligence Process

- Be careful with regard to confidentiality agreements and NDAs. You will need to get express permission to discuss what you are doing or thinking of doing with the tech company especially if you have signed an NDA with them.

- The problem is not that these VCs are aligned with the tech giants necessarily, though many of the investors and advisors in their organizations are in fact ex-Facebook, ex-Google, ex-IBM Microsoft and so on. That is already a warning bell with regard to confidentiality and for that reason alone the entrepreneurs may withhold their permission. Increasingly, the VCs you meet are former entrepreneurs who have told their innovative emerging tech to a larger competitor or established corporation.

- More to the point, their trade secrets if shared with you may be passed on (wrongly) to a competitor venture that is in stealth mode and not yet visible. That means that this hidden venture could be incubating inside the VCs' pipeline for deal flow or already have received funding and is in R&D about to go to market.

- That could be fatal for the tech venture you want to give a chance to! You could also be sued for breaching the NDA or confidentiality implied if you discuss too freely with competitors or experts funding these potential future or currently hidden competitors. Just because you and your peers may not have heard of this innovation until now, it is quite likely the trend of the innovation had already been spotted years ago by their talent and trend scouts at the private equity firm. That is their job and how they make money, they want to be first movers!

- However the sad fact is, it is frequently very hard for boot-strapped, unheard of ventures to win capital investment from these big investors in an early stage of business development. That is why you will feel like you are entering a world of smokescreens, cloak and daggers.

- It is high stakes. We are talking about "pre money" ventures worth tens of millions of dollars before they have their first paying customer or show profits—for high-profit ground-breaking innovation. And it is often about strategic positioning and strategic communications. Which is why it is so hard for you to make purchasing decision.

- This vicious circle will always present itself with really new, exciting, innovative technologies. You will need to scratch below the surface to get the information and do the due diligence you will need to do to commit to a six-month pilot or longer. Anything less is of less value and not really viable for the tech entrepreneur in terms of marketing, new client acquisition, and using you as a crucial testimonial from a first-mover client.

Approach any competitor to your entrepreneurs or any corporate-sponsored expert with extreme caution. I used to think what has a tech giant got to be afraid of? The reality is, none of the dominant players ever want to lose even a slice of their market share even to a minnow like a completely unknown, unmonetized early stage venture run by unpaid cofounders.

Sadly, too many tech giants and their past and present executives are known to act badly even unethically to stop an innovative tech company in its tracks. They do not want the slightest bit of competition. If the startup survives as a new venture—gets traction on the market as the jargon goes—and becomes a serious threat to the giant's market share, then they will bid to acquire it more often than not. This is called an M&A, a merger and acquisition whereby the new venture is basically taken over by the old.

But until that point, a truly disruptive and innovative tech venture must strategically guard its first-mover client list, its marketing strategies, even the names of its team. Given these life-and-death sensitivities, you must be ethical at all times and check with the entrepreneurs about who they are comfortable with regards to you checking on them. A big competitor's name attached to an expert's salary or organization should signal a big red flag for you in this context.

Phase 3: Nurturing and Managing Your Chosen Bot Developers

Remember at the beginning of this textbook I discussed what is happening in the public sector in Britain. Specifically at the UK Department for Workplace and Pensions and their multibillion pound budget to roll out chatbots and AI. I know from firsthand experience that they have been talking with external bot developers about plugging in chatbots from the private sector, adapted to their public service needs. So I was curious to read shortly before Brexit Eve as I name the end of October 2019, that the DWP had decided to establish a high-powered, extensive intrapreneurship department and centers around the country.

> The DWP is also rapidly expanding its own private technology company, Benefits and Pensions Digital Technology Services Ltd, which recruited more than 400 staff in the year to April, while DWP Digital recruited 520.
>
> A spokesperson for the DWP insisted it was using artificial intelligence to help people find work, to reduce the burden on claimants to prove their circumstances, and to help vulnerable people access welfare more easily without having to provide evidence of their digital identity.[1]

This DWP example is a clear case of public sector procurement, not of external entrepreneurs to commission botification services, but recruiting intrapreneurs or new full-time staff to conceptualize, develop, and realize greenfield projects and pilots from within the multitude of governmental organizations that make up the Department or Ministry.

Alternatively you can choose a tech venture from outside your company who you want to bring in and run a greenfield project. Alternatively, some companies are "sourcing entrepreneurs and coders" themselves and giving them short-term contracts to develop an application from within the company.

I think there is an erroneous belief that creating your own startup from inside your organization somehow gives you more control and security. However, there are many pitfalls with this type of intrapreneurship, and I cover these points in the following. For both entrepreneurs outside your company providing the pilot, and the intrapreneurs doing R&D

---

[1] "March of the 'welfare robot' triggers fears for poorest". p. 19. The Guardian October 15, 2019. Robert Booth. Social affairs correspondent. Front page story and pp. 18–19.

for a project within your organization the following points should be considered:

- Set realistic milestones.
- Be flexible and fair on deadlines.
- Keep communication lines open at all time.
- Be reliable in giving feedback on time, tell them if you don't understand something—it can be fatal to a project to not admit your failure to comprehend any detail or overall description of the collaboration and it creates an unnecessary working atmosphere of friction and potentially resentment.
- Get your team and managers to give feedback after each milestone where possible.

Dealing With External Entrepreneurs for Projects Created and Run Externally

- Keep the media away until the AB testing has been completed to the venture's satisfaction and yours.
- Discuss with the entrepreneurs how you want the media coverage and future external comms (communications, media liaison, marketing, PR) to be handled, how they are to be portrayed, and what is their tech story.
- Work out a PR and marketing strategy with your resident marketers and comms directors so they don't feel cut out of the loop. They will probably need to give you and the project sign off, not just your bosses.
- Communicate clearly to all stakeholders at every point what the expectations are and where there are delays explain why, don't cover them up, that is, don't not communicate the issues in a timely, fair way.
- Most people understand pilots will have unexpected problems. Given the tech venture is operating externally to your company or organization, the entrepreneurs will inevitably be working on other prototypes and pitching to other first-mover

clients, if not already working on several pilots in parallel. That is inevitable if you are not paying them for this work or paying little.

- If you don't like the fact they are not focused on your company's pilot, then you may have to sign an exclusivity contract which negotiates their time and how long it should be devoted to your pilot alone. Entrepreneurs will want to be paid (extra possibly) for this.
- However, don't expect the external tech venture to give you exclusivity over their technology! That is an anti-competitive ask that should be rewarded or compensated for monetarily, without question or much argument.
- If you want them to not offer the innovative solution to your competitors, you will have to put a higher payment clause in the contract, that is, so the entrepreneurs are not put at a financial disadvantage giving up other clients and contracts to focus only on you.
- Intellectual property lawyers will probably get involved then to calculate the worth of the tech now and in [the period of time for the exclusivity] and arrive at a pricing range that is fair to the entrepreneurs.
- It is not a monopoly situation if this payment system for exclusivity is agreed upon as a fair exchange to give the paying client a first-mover advantage over their competitors who have been too slow to adopt the new tech of the entrepreneurs.

For Intrapreneurs

- Encourage positivity and optimism for all involved.
- If people at your company are unduly negative and skeptical, call them out on this attitude. Get them to do the quiz at the start of Chapter 4, ask them if they are an advocate of new technologies or an opponent.
- Nipping it in the bud can prevent a mobbing type of effect at the launch date where if something goes wrong, the company doesn't hit the panic button and kill off the innovative project

without proper consideration and reasoned planning, for example, agreeing on a postponed second release with new milestones and budgets.

- Where hired coders are working nine-to-five on your internal pilot and R&D in an intrapreneurship situation (like the DWP's new business and staff), those time constraints in themselves turn it into an office job rather than a startup. Don't be surprised if progress becomes slower than with tech entrepreneurs driven and motivated by ownership of their intellectual property, the reward of profits and dividends and building a business (scaling up) on their own outside the company.

- For this reason, it might be useful to have as an early milestone to spin out the pilot as a standalone venture, that is, register it independently of your company so that the coders and business development managers have a sense of ownership and autonomous control. Many universities operate in this way have full-time salaried commercialization or knowledge transfer manager to shepherd this process. Even to IPO stage for a university spin out company that gets seed funding from its university. Note that means the entrepreneurs/academics often lose the full ownership of their intellectual property, which is then shared with the university as its business angel providing the incubator environment for them.

- This might sound scary for large corporations and some SMEs, however this has become common practice for R&D projects with proven traction and promise of relatively fast commercialization to become their own companies as spinouts (UK) and spinoff (U.S.) from the parent company.

- It is a term most frequently used for university and business school lab experiments and long-term research that gathers momentum.

- The academic structure usually provides a unit of specialists to supervise spinning out these ventures mostly created by their own students, graduates, and academic staff.

- Like the university version, as corporate investors in your own spin out ventures, you ought to look carefully at the intellectual property arrangements—who owns the IP if the innovation began "inhouse"? If the coder team says it was their invention, who else can claim that it wasn't?
- In the last century, this problem was mostly solved with employment contracts stipulating that all of the R&D belonged to the "corporation as investor" who hired them to be intrapreneurs.
- However, today with the rapidity of inventions and convergence, it may be very hard to find the most talented people who will agree to these conditions that they forgo the innovation they may be responsible for in a small coding team.
- For the sake of motivation, it may be useful to offer them part ownership and shareholder stakes in the company, especially if they succeed in spinning out the invention into a separate company from the "mother corporation" that you all work for as salaried employees and/or as contractors.

Government Procurement Checklist

- Have you checked with the relevant departments if they have anything in the pipeline for trialing this technology?
- Don't assume there is nothing happening it may not have been communicated yet—the good old silo divisions often prevent knowledge being shared.
- Ask the HR head if they know of any initiatives.
- Where possible circulate a call or e-newsletter for ideas and feedback at the planning stage; ask to meet in the canteen individually or if there is a strong response, suggest an "AI lunch" or whatever topic once a month after work or lunchtime to generate staff "buy in" and crowdsource their ideas ongoing.
- If you work for a large corporation, government, or an international NGO, check with the company's librarians and

Figure 5.4 © *Realfiction, Copenhagen, 2019. This is a perfect example of Augmented Reality imaging in Real Time being used to promote a product or brand. With the addition of Cognitive Interfaces in future, such as AI notifaction with voice, the AR experience of just seeing a car like this in commercial setting will become a more interactive branding experience. Voice tech will let shoppers chat with the car itself or its human hologram ambassador or sales rep*

archivists for literature and records of past pilots and current policy papers for implementing the emerging tech fields you want to trial.

- Ask your managers what they think regarding the current policies and planning.
- Ask your junior staff and colleagues from other departments about their plans for new tech to see if there is overlap and potential for interdepartmental collaboration that you haven't thought of yet.
- Publicize the proposed implementation date on the staff e-newsletter.
- Ask colleagues if they have heard of the ventures and/or entrepreneurs on your shortlist.
- Check with the government funding agencies if they know of them or can recommend any new tech startups as suppliers.

- Compare your goals and plans with other countries and their ministries or departments; you will be surprised by the similarities and learn from the differences.
- Where there is a similar project done or underway in another country, contact your counterpart ask for a video conference call to share experiences.
- Check with university researchers, business schools, and institutes.
- As a government official or civil servant, you are best to avoid going to the tech giants or established companies for peer reviews—see the previous discussion. This will by nature not be neutral as their goal is to demolish any incumbents as legacy systems—they don't want their market share disrupted.
- Similarly, you must be careful about talking with VCs and consultants who will inevitably have vested interests in companies they already own or have invested in. They are obviously going to present their proteges as your best bet and cannot be relied upon to declare this conflict of interest. Sad but true in today's world of shaky business ethics!

Special Considerations for Government Decision Makers

- Follow the same due diligence steps as the aforementioned corporate checklists and be aware of the pitfalls in sourcing reliable information about unknown tech.
- When asking for information from other related government agencies it may not be forthcoming. Even other departments at your level of government, for example, Council, Local, County, State, Federal, or national may also be defensive if they have missed a trend or not been agile enough to spot it. Or else they are plain old opponents of new tech, as per the quiz in this book!
- Often semigovernment experts have become too comfortable and reluctant to make any fundamental changes like adopting

new tech, especially (ironically) if they are in funding agencies like grants and government financing schemes.

- They have so many eager entrepreneurs wanting to pitch to them desperate for funds, that some government officials and civil servants may rest on their laurels and are quick to cover up their deficiencies, lack of knowledge of current trends, and overstate their past achievements.

- Coverups and nondisclosure of similar tests and trials of the same technology or related innovations may occur because they were flops. It is human nature to want to downplay failures you may be personally or indirectly responsible for. In government, this unwillingness can reach epic proportions as they have different dynamics for disclosing departmental incidents and somewhat secretive protocols for not sharing information, even with colleagues.

- In the private sector, the financial necessity of profits and economies of scale is the determining factor. People are reluctant to withhold information because it will soon come to light that they caused a failure due to a lack of information sharing.

- Tech ventures in the early stages are usually lean and mean operations of five people, sometimes a team of ten. There is nowhere to hide and so accountability in disclosing to your colleagues failed attempts or "accounts lost" is almost guaranteed. Or you will find your contract terminated abruptly. A lean and mean startup has no time to lose, and no money to waste due to staff's personal feelings of discomfort about failure.

- Check with industry experts you respect but do not tell them who are you are checking on due to the anti-competitive clauses in your nondisclosure agreement with the external entrepreneurs. It is just general good practice in the highly competitive world of launching innovation.

- See the aforementioned checklist for corporate purchasers which goes in depth into this aspect. I have not applied it to the same extent to the public sector because in my experience, there is more awareness of—and openly strict rules for—public servants for discretion and following the departmental guidelines on purchasing.

- Civil servants are employed on the basis of neutrality, which is enforced by strict codes of conduct and also internal guidelines for procurement and tenders for suppliers, that is, most governments have separate units dedicated to sourcing providers and suppliers according to strict, public procurement guidelines to avoid corruption, bribery and favoritism in public and/or political office.

For Both the Public and Private Sectors

Key Advice

------- Original Message -------
On Thursday, October 17, 2019 13:20, Jon <jon@leftfieldmedia.com. au> wrote:

I agree with, 'I bet nobody has even mentioned it at all to the Top Dog'!

And having been in this position myself, multiple times, what you said about, 'It's simply not fair to start ups to make them repeat pitches over and over to different silos', is just so, so true.

Startups who are being starved of oxygen and who don't have the luxury of time on their sides, and have a critical need to gain traction and commercialize their product.

Not too pushy at all Tania, in fact I think you have struck a nice balance between stating the facts, and presenting the benefits to him here.

Sent from my Left Field Interactive Media iPhone while on the move ...

This e-mail between our Head of Asia Pacific Sales in Melbourne, Jon Field, and myself sitting on a farm in Kent, chasing deals globally online, sums it all up really.[2] Be fair to entrepreneurs, they are usually working nearly 20 hours a day on average.

When you don't become their internal advocate after you are convinced they have an innovation your company should adopt, you are wearing them out with needless pitches and meetings. Startup owners make these sessions comfortable and easy for you, that is their job. Behind the scenes, it takes enormous energy and resources to make just these corporate pitches happen, often on a shoestring or nonexistent budget.

Here are some more tips on how you can make your entrepreneurial journey more pleasurable and better prepared for all those involved, even down to your company's inhouse maintenance staff who may have the mundane task of installing the electrical and Internet connections for the device or mixed reality experience:

- Watch videos on YouTube and TED conference talks relevant to what you want to implement.
- If time allows, go to as many conferences and tech trade shows as possible, ask to be introduced to leading speakers who have been paid to be there, not the other way around. Sadly the business model of most trade shows and tech conferences is that the companies with the biggest marketing budgets pay the organizers to put them on stage. And then everyone pretends they are not listening to veiled advertisement.
- Be clear on what you want to achieve and how you are going to publicize it in relation to your brand, your department, your company, or organization, so that the entrepreneurs understand their role in the media plan and what confidentiality levels are required.
- If journalists and tech editors get wind of your pilot somehow and start contacting you, for example, is the government going to replace civil servants with robots? Is corporation X going to use artificial intelligence instead of business analysts,

---

[2] E-mail communication with the author and Jon Field, Melbourne, October 17, 2019, on behalf of AI Bots as a Service UG, Munich.

chatbots instead of call centers, digitization and remote working instead of offices and a headquarters, then you may need to prepare a response. No comment may be taken as assent in some media.

- Work this out with your organization media team and the wishes of the entrepreneurs if they are external, and intrapreneurs if they have been recruited to work for you inhouse on an R&D greenfield project.

Guidelines for AI Apps: Understanding What You Want and Measuring It

Dos and Don'ts

- Cybersecurity—make sure all the parties involved have covered the anti-hacking measures adequately to prevent hackers or malware entering or spreading from your pilot.
- Data protection—getting an MOU (Memorandum of Understanding) signed that has clauses stating who is liable for data breaches under GDPR is essentially all you need to do here. But best to check this!
- Respecting the creative work and IP of the tech venture at all times, as much as possible either by actions, word or written praise of milestones achieved together.
- Acknowledge the commercial value of this emerging tech with payment if possible. If this is an unpaid pilot on the basis of an exchange of marketing campaigns in return for the trial of technology, then make sure you keep your end of the bargain and promote the startup's innovation clearly and reliably to their satisfaction.
- Be a reliable partner—communicate what is going on and don't leave the team hanging in radio silence. They are working in underfunded, pressurized environments!

- Give fair testimonials—you can put an early stage venture out of business within a week if you give unfair criticism to a prospective new client.
- Scaling up for a startup is a slow and painful process so you are in a privileged position of power over their future and past investment. Be mindful and don't abuse your power to put a rapid end to their innovation.
- Don't lose patience, remember the extreme conditions these entrepreneurs are working under—no pay, or inadequately paid for years to do R&D, and bootstrapping their venture under pressure of cash flow issues and trying to fund new client acquisitions.
- Don't reveal secrets to competitors, even if these competitors are "famous" established brands who approach you directly or indirectly to gather business intelligence or even to try to steal the contract away from the startup you are nurturing. Stay committed and keep your integrity intact by not divulging any details to the Goliaths of industry.
- Encourage them in entrepreneurship and acknowledge the many sacrifices they have made to get their tech to market, both in their personal life and their professional life, for example, they have forgone a highly paid, full-time salary like yours!

General Guidelines When Botifying Websites, Databases, and Public Spaces

When commissioning a 2D chatbot for online deployment (usually on an Instant Messaging platform), or if you want to be a pioneer in the 3D Mixed Reality avatar space, AI bot holograms or Virtual Reality/AR experiences, then you should make sure you consider all of these points:

- Privacy
- Data protection
- Contextual practices and cultural expectations
- Demographic expectations

Figure 5.5 © *Realfiction, Copenhagen, 2019. To date, Augmented Reality and Virtual Reality have not botified the experience. The interaction has been created through gesture as you see here. The man is waving at the AR image to select a color button. Once the gesture is understood by the AR software, it will change the color of the car for the shopper. Voice commands is the next interactive step, as is the "implanting" of a bot brain which my company AI BaaS is currently doing in our HQ in Munich and Mixed Reality lab in Devon, UK*

- User habits
- Defined consumers
- Random exchanges
- Unpredictable interactions
- Website are less used than apps
- Most people, anywhere in the world, only use a maximum of five apps on their phone on a regular basis
- Therefore Instant Messaging is and will be the preferred medium of communication between people and brands
- Social media and installations, for example, immersive reality.

CHAPTER 6

Conclusion

Support the Local Economy, Regional Infrastructure, and National Productivity Goals

There is a strong case to be made that as Procurement and Purchasing specialists and decision makers, you should put your immediate goals for your company or government body in the wider context of innovation development. How did this innovation come to be? Was it from your immediate regional infrastructure in terms of a tech hub, incubator, or accelerator that has been largely funded by taxpayers' money? Is the new venture a privately owned startup with transparency over who owns the intellectual property? Or is it a spin-out from a large corporation or a university, which means the entrepreneurs do not necessarily own the IP completely?

These factors matter because it is easy enough to Spend Other People's Money—in this case the budget you have been allocated by your department, unit or boss—on a surefire brand that everybody knows. Without mentioning names here, it is a low risk option to just sign for the package that comes from a big name Software as a Service provider that is omnipresent. What could go wrong?

You need to reframe the way you look at purchasing innovation and put it in terms of payoff: I take more risk but can always justify it with the knowledge that it has created jobs in the local economy. It has put my company or government body in good stead with the regional infrastructure providers, for example, local government services and Chambers of Commerce/business groups because we have bought from local sellers rather than foreign companies that may not even pay corporate tax in your country, so no trickled down into funding the said infrastructure and tech hubs!

Above all, you can reframe your purchasing decision in terms of national productivity goals. What is that tangibly speaking and put into your everyday office life and work routine? Well, let's focus on the example of emails and chatbots. As we have seen in this book, many business intelligence firms are picking chatbots or IVAs as the future of communications, which inevitably makes emailing redundant, if it is not already so in many aspects.

Chatbots Are the Future According To a Londoner Lobby Platform and The Mayor in 2019

The following extract from the CognitionX Taster White Paper 2019 makes it very clear that "most chatbot deployment plans are in the next year or so, most chatbot plans expect substantial investment and impact, the use of natural language is expected to grow substantially."[1] We need to take their research seriously because although CogX is a relatively new AI bots platform campaigning to support the UK niche industry, it has support at the highest levels of government, which is all important in the British economic context.

It has been backed by the London mayor Sadiq Khan who spoke at their annual conference in the capital in summer 2019. And it has the express backing of the current UK government through CogX's high profile cofounder Tabitha Goldenstaub from Wimbledon and a successful serial entrepreneur. Goldstaub has a powerful reputation as a feminist in the tech world, visibly campaigning to get more women into STEM and especially into artificial intelligence companies in order to reduce algorithmic bias in its development and commercial roll-out.

As the previous CogX excerpt summarizes, chatbots will be taking over the world! It describes the "future of chatbots as ubiquitous, much like speech in humans." Just as well because as we can see from this American use case as shown in the following, even absolutely necessary business or educational human conversations are far from guaranteed with the next generation(s), partly the fault of technology and partly solved by it.

---

[1] file:///C:/Users/Andrew/Downloads/Chatbots_and_Voicebots-Teaser-v3.pdf

Figure 6.1 © Realfiction, Copenhagen, 2019. The Danish manufacturer of this frame that creates 3D hologram experiences like this dinosaur skeleton suddenly coming to life, is a pioneer in CX tech. The Customer Experience, even for visitors to a natural history museum, has reached a new bar of expectations and consumer satisfaction. Mixed Reality experiences like this one is providing a benchmark for user interaction or UX

Boston's Botification of University Campuses for Next-Gen Humans

Let's look at the excellent statistics of this Boston-based challenger tech company AdmitHub. Full disclosure: I met the cofounder Andrew Maggioli at the Re-Work Deep Learning Summit, their inaugural Chatbots Track, end of 2016. I enjoyed Andrew's case studies he shared during his keynote and have followed AdmitHub's exponential growth since then admiringly given they have forged ahead despite all the misconceptions about 2D chatbots as discussed in this book. They have convinced enough users in their vertical of higher education of their specific use case.

The point here about productivity is that AdmitHub's research has found that Generation Z only opens 20 percent of the emails sent to them by the higher education administrators, the Admissions Centers, their lecturers, and the associated university service providers.[2] That represents a staggering 80 percent loss in productivity for this student–admin communication! I have heard this pain point repeated by UK, Australian, French, and German higher education operators who have come to my company AI Bots as a Service for Requests for Proposals, so it definitely is a global trend.

This means for the precious university budgets—again largely taxpayer and government funded in most advanced economies—large amounts are being wasted on communicating students who ignore these communications. What should they do? Send out pigeons and smoke signals to the recalcitrant Gen Zers? Interrupt their Wi-Fi on campus to broadcast Official News and comms like in the Golden Days of 1950s television and radio alerts to the nation before that?

The answer lies in chatbots because the 2D bots are in the medium that Gen Z does engage with: texting or more accurately Instant Messaging. AdmitHub has published a white paper asserting that as opposed to the ignoring of 80 percent of emails sent to them, 98 percent university or college students will open and read text messages or IM notifications, and do so more or less immediately. Radically in terms of productive communications and the massive resources spent in terms of staff, time, and organization on campus, 40 percent of Gen Z students will also reply to the administrators' messages!

AdmitHub has cleverly integrated this emerging data into their sales pitch and I note the majority of its Bostonian staff are sales and marketing account managers. Their 2D AI bots they are now calling their chatbot solution can help with that 40 percent conversion rate and restore some element of productivity to student–administrator communications.

Let's face it—less than one-fifth of your target audience even reading what you say about something as important as their upcoming exam dates, changes of rooms, exam results, and admission info can only be considered an unproductive waste of time. Chatbots to the rescue in that at least they will get the message through and have double the chance of obtaining a response, a reaction if not an action from the target of the comms.

---

[2] https://admithub.com/resources/guide-for-engaging-gen-z/

Entrepreneurial, Intrapreneurial, and the Sales Dead End

As we have seen in the previous checklists section, a different approach is required for entrepreneurs engaged with outside of your organization as opposed to recruiting intrapreneurs, that is, new recruits hired to run a pilot from within your company. If you misstep and end the pilot, it could be the end of the venture externally. You could have just killed off a startup in the public domain. Bad kudos for you and word gets around in the tech scene you are a partner/purchaser to avoid. Naming and shaming can happen these days very indiscreetly, but it does happen.

Closing down an internal R&D unit is another matter. Financial risk is often absolutely minimized by being forced to operate in a predefined budget, with money "given" to the intrapreneurial team before they even startup in their allocated office space. A comfortable feeling of being nurtured and removing the enormous stress of bootstrapping and "having to find the money to cover costs somehow" also removes the urgency that is lived and breathed in a normal startup scenario.

So ending that pilot you have created as a greenfield project causes less financial pain to the intrapreneurs because they are, after all, salaried

Figure 6.2 © Realfiction Copenhagen, 2019. This dinosaur is an example of an animated life-sized hologram. This type of Mixed Reality is the multimedia format used by AI BaaS to "implant various bot brains" effectively turning the giant hardware device into a shell or physical framework for a live, organically developing Cognitive Interface

staff and have the emotional security of knowing when the next paycheck arrives. And being notified ahead of time that their pay will end if the project has "failed" or is discontinued.

Often these team members will be redeployed by HR to other parts of the company and have become more "employable" by virtue of having done this pilot project with famous Brand X or established Company Y. The kudos of having been paid to experiment puts them in a good place in the employment market as many of them will be "strategically recruited" to new ventures that are scaling up. So those who are prepared to take more financial risks and be in a less secure form of employment in a startup—perhaps already backed by VCs or a business angel, or otherwise existing on first revenues—will usually have a choice of positions in the startup ecosystem.

My comments on someone's personal, cultural, ethnic, and psychological attitude to risk-taking and ability to adapt to pressurized situations for long period of times will greatly determine whether an intrapreneur converts to a full-time salary or contract employee status instead of staying in the permanently fluctuating, ever uncertain emerging tech scene. Even if you do end up with a C-suite title and there are less than five of you in the business! More work, more flexibility, more control over the business development, and hopefully resulting in more financial benefits and direct payment "rewards" in return for the hectic lifestyle.

Both have a sales dead end though the intrapreneurs are better protected. A startup winding down or ending suddenly could mean the entrepreneurs lose their house, car, and savings. That is the meaning of risk, sweat equity, and skin in the game!

As this book makes clear with reference to many case studies where enormous amounts of work and preparation went into requests for proposals, presentations, contract negotiations, and readiness to begin the project yet ended abruptly in a "sales dead end," this can be fatal for many entrepreneurs. Corporate purchasers and civil service procurement units must, at all times, be aware that they are engaging with high-value innovators in society. They are to be respected for that fact alone. And treated with courtesy when communicating the probability of projects being approved—and paid for—or the reasons as to why they may not.

Sadly in today's society globally, new ventures are routinely "used and abused" by both the public and private sectors. Many like big public broadcasters, telcos, energy corporations, state-run infrastructure like transport or large banks have endless funds to keep R&D units going and growing for decades on end. With very few results when you compare their careful, cautious greenfield experiments with the do-or-die soft launches and big splashes of startups on a shoestring. These intrapreneurs often "lead on" or falsely engage their emerging competitors outside of their organization, promising to license their niche innovation and pay them for their software or device.

However, I must flag the sad circumstance—from hearsay and personal experience—that nine times out of ten, these trusting young ventures are exploited for their knowhow, ideas, and often blatantly their intellectual property. It is copied by the salaried intrapreneurs or else modified and sourced elsewhere "cheaper" by executives who think having to deal directly with apparently freewheeling, overly passionate entrepreneurs is too much hassle and potentially an irreparable loss of status for them personally if things go belly up down the track.

Looking back over my 20 years in this startup ecosystem space, from Berlin to Sydney, London to San Francisco, Melbourne to Singapore, France to Africa and the overarching dominance of a seemingly unassailable U.S. tech giants, at times working in unison like a cartel in terms of internet presence and pricing, countered only by comparatively few, equally opaque, technology monopolizing monoliths coming out of China, Japan, and South Korea, I can see how innovation has been shamelessly stifled.

The U.S. Democrat leader Elisabeth Wilson and her cohort have rightfully called for U.S. tech giants to be curtailed in their power to destroy and obstruct even fledgling competitors. In fact, Facebook openly admits they have a "radar system" to detect any emergent threat coming from the global startup ecosystem that could take even a fraction of a fraction of their market share away.

We see the fast-acting, smothering actions of other tech giants belonging to the FAANGs when a threat emerges from a city's ecosystem, as most hubs of entrepreneurship are now developed per city and via regional infrastructure. They buy up the promising startup and put it in their stable of young unknowns. The M&A of a small company by a giant corporation is universally portrayed in the mainstream media as a triumph, and a commercialization success story for the respective government that has poured millions of taxpayers' money into building the tech hub the M&A took place in.

How sad it is that the next generation of innovators are being told by their official government funders, the state-sponsored business advisers, their tech solicitors, accountants, and above all their ecosystem peers that the ultimate goal and measure of success is to be bought by an invariably American corporation? What happened to aspiring to be a family-owned company run for generations? What about making the innovation and all the decades of resources, unpaid, used to create the USP, pay for itself by keeping the company going yourselves?

What about aspiring to become an SME or *KMU* part of the *Mittelstand* (middle sector) as it is called, quite respectfully and often admiringly, in Germany? Even a listing on the public stock exchanges seems to have been removed as an achievable milestone in the hope you might just be merged or acquired instead. And be considered a smart winner for having the nous to cash in on your hard work and endless hours of your seven day week to get your venture "over the line."

It signals a loss of confidence in the robustness of your intellectual property, if you prefer to sell out to a big competitor rather than keep the company going and make it a challenger to the tech giants. Sure, they sabotage and make life tough for you as small fry in the global economy. But I think this issue has to be raised among us. From the buyer and seller side, the innovators and the purchasers need innovation to thrive and grow in the technological age of Industry 4.0.

If the tech entrepreneurs are all too willing to hand over their IP and proprietary algorithms at the drop of a hat to a giant competitor, where will the diversity of the market and drive for competitive prices and quality improvements come from?

Following is an excerpt from Jonathan Reichental's list of five things to consider for the "future of government services." He and his coauthor of this paper have identified what makes best practices for government procurement and above all, governmental adoption of new tech.[3] The first two "recommended behaviors" for civil servants and government officials are (a) leadership and (b) vision. Here is what Reichental and Choudhury say about the other best practices and leading examples of where they are applied: Estonia in the EU, Dubai in the Middle East, and the United Arab Emirates (UAE)

3. Experimentation

In our research we have found that agencies that have great constituent experiences, are also open to experimentation of ideas. They prototype and pilot. They try different approaches. They take more risk. They also recognize that failure is an option and if they do fail, they learn and then move forward. Experimentation is a favorable behavior and a contributing factor in almost all successful innovation.

4. Cocreation

Great organizations build solutions together with their customers. They bring them in early, they experiment and design together, and then they deploy together. All stakeholders, internal and external, take responsibility when there is success and humbly accept when things don't work out right. In the government, bringing in constituents to cocreate solutions adds enormous value to the process. At a minimum, they will likely have great ideas that haven't been considered from the perspective of the government agency, and they will be able to guide the process of enhancing the customer journey.

5. Action

Finally, an agency can have all the leadership and vision it needs, but if it doesn't have a disposition for action, it's all for nothing. Sure, action has risk and there are always many reasons to defer, stall, and post-

[3] https://reichental.com/?p=1548 POSTED IN BIG THOUGHTS GENERAL TECHNOLOGY GOVERNMENT INNOVATION. The Future of Government Services, Part 4. October 2, 2019 - 2:21 pm By Dr. Jonathan Reichental, CEO, Human Future, and Chetan Choudhury, Government Adviser .

pone. But action is where, well, where the action is! Agencies with a proclivity for doing things, even when the outcome is more uncertain than they would like, move the ball forward. A vision for high quality government experiences requires a lot of action versus a bureaucratic approach that plagues most government entities.

The Future

There are many examples to point to, but we particularly think the e-service work in Estonia reflects the five behaviors we've identified. They provide the best outcome of a deliberate effort to change the game in government experiences. Another good example can be cited from the work happening in Dubai and Abu Dhabi in the United Arab Emirates (UAE) where the government is leading from the front in enhancing the customer experience around services using multiple techniques like mystery shopping, cocreation, experimentation, proto-typing, service bundling based on life events, and more.

Sure, the situations in Estonia or UAE have their own uniqueness, but our five behaviors are not aligned with any particular culture or circumstance. In fact, we recognize that these five behaviors can be applied in a wide variety of contexts. Use them liberally.

There's a remarkable opportunity all over the world to change how people engage with government. It's not only essential for better outcomes, but it's what constituents would like to experience. The tools, techniques, and talent exist. What remains is a choice.

At the World Government Summit in Dubai in February this year, leaders from around the world discussed these challenges at a government services forum. You can read the report of that discussion here: https://gx.ae/en/resources/government-services-forum-at-the-world-government-summit-2019-detailed-report

Afterword

As I finish writing this book at the end of autumn 2019, I look back on my physical and virtual journeys while working on it for the past year or so. Almost in a "multiverse" sense! As an ad hoc subscriber to the Posthumanism school of thought, where IT innovation can optimistically improve our daily lives and introduce Equal Opportunity rather than destroy it, I am also a mystic in the sense of the Japanese and their Shintoism, which allows them to form meaningful relationships with not just AI-infused robots and objects but the spiritual forces of nature.

More and more people are making the connection between Shintoism and a way to "deal with" AI-powered entities, such as the BBC's Aleks Krotoski in her Digital Human Series episode on "Animism:"[4]

> Aleks Krotoski explores our anxieties around AI and automation. Comparing western philosophy to that of the east, she'll ask if some of fears around technology are cultural. Much of western thinking is still strongly influenced by Christian traditions which places humanity at the top of the tree of creation. We rebel against anything that challenges that. Whether it be Galileo telling us we're not the center of the universe or Darwin telling us we're nothing more than shaved monkeys.

> It can be argued that the invention of AI is just that sort of challenge to our supremacy. But in Japan they see things very differently; Shintoism leads to a philosophy without the Christian hierarchy. In their "creation" everything is alive and connected to everything else. Just like the modern digital world. What can we learn from looking at technology differently.

I share the "general public's" concerns about how the unchecked, that is, unregulated roll out of Artificial Intelligence applications can be detrimental for large segments of a country's population. In Chapter 2 with the first case study, I raised the alarm of what happens when we get chatbots influencing humans during an election campaign. This has now been proven to be the case with the noncompromising Zealot Bots as named by University of Cambridge researchers.[5]

---

[4] Krotoski, A. 2019. "Animism." *The Digital Human Series, BBC*, October 21, 2019, https://bbc.co.uk/programmes/m0009kyy

[5] https://ft.com/content/c3b7486a-d2eb-11e9-8d46-8def889b4137

The Guardian's expose, as discussed earlier in this book, has pointed to the international creation of a "digital poorhouse" that is being created by the governments of the United States, UK, Australia, and India primarily, according to their investigative journalism.[6] It is not so much the robotic form of humanoid robots like Pepper running amok or playing with our emotions and manipulating humans, as in the 2019 German cult classic documentary *Hi, AI* so cleverly presented to us in narrative filmic form, rather it is the AI-powered applications like facial recognition and data mining that causes me sleepless nights.

Facial recognition unchecked, as the UK Civil Liberties groups have determined by calling out police use of it without the public's awareness, and even corporate use of facial recognition on the streets around Kings Cross and London—maybe elsewhere in the UK, who knows?—is now on the agenda of Civil Rights organizations to fight within their own countries, not abroad in developing or poor countries where we normally expect human rights to be broached if not consistently abused. They are taking their cause to the TV talk shows and the internet social media forums. Facial recognition technology's main problem is its low success rate or big failure to correctly identify people. For that reason, it has recently been banned by the U.S. authorities in policing because it cannot reliably identify criminals and/or distinguish between the sought target and ordinary members of the public.

Do you know you are under surveillance by AI-powered software? If not, how can you find out? The starting point is obviously all the surveillance issues surrounding the tech giants and social media companies' use of our personal data and private messaging. For me the biggest risks are social manipulation and deskilling of humans—basic "skills" like raising children and how to vote, things that are so private and public but never been disrupted in a negative way to the core.

In the autumn of 2019, a backlash about Amazon Alexa was unleashed by a reportage on Channel 4 news about how Alexa reading bedtime

---

[6] PilKington, E. 2019. "Digital Dystopia: How Algorithms Punish the Poor." Automating Poverty series. Analysis from New York. *The Guardian*, October 14, 2019, https://theguardian.com/technology/2019/oct/14/automating-poverty-algorithms-punish-poor

stories to kids had contributed to them "not knowing what a book is or how to use it" as well as their poor verbal skills such as speaking in a whole sentence or even in an intelligible way. As the articles echoing the Channel 4 report show, four- and five-year-olds were looking at their peers conversant in the English language for their age group "as if they were not understanding foreigners." Quite shockingly, even for me as an industry expert, these kids were trying to swipe books as they did not know about turning pages.

I am focusing on this broadsheet, the working class *Daily Mail* coverage, for several reasons. The "scandal" was heralded by the supposedly "intellectual's choice of news delivery," Channel 4 news. However, as I explain in the following, it wasn't, tragically, really news at all in Britain.

News Headline: Parents' reliance on AI means some children are starting school unable to speak in sentences as it emerges many are even being read bedtime stories by devices like Alexa

Parents' reliance on AI means some children are starting school unable to speak in sentences as it emerges many are even being read bedtime stories by devices like Alexa

- **Reception teachers have children starting school not knowing how to use books**
- **One teacher even claimed more than half their intake cannot speak in sentences**
- **Another claimed that children now go to sleep after Alexa reads them a story**

Children are being read bedtime stories by Alexa and are starting school unable to speak in sentences, teachers warn.

A survey found that families are relying on the virtual assistant to entertain their children—while some four and five-year-olds try to 'swipe' books as they are so addicted to mobile phones.

---

[7] Sarah Harris, *Daily Mail* September 20, 2019, https://dailymail.co.uk/news/article-7484189/Parents-reliance-AI-means-children-starting-school-unable-speak-sentences.html

The findings were revealed in a poll of 100 reception teachers about pupils who started school this month.

One teacher said more than half their intake 'cannot speak in sentences or be reliably understood by adults'. Another told researchers many children 'now go to sleep with a story from Alexa rather than a parent' [File photo]

Eighty-two per cent said "increasing numbers of children aren't adequately prepared to start school."

The same proportion claim there are more speech and language issues than five years ago.

One teacher said more than half their intake "cannot speak in sentences or be reliably understood by adults."

Some 72 per cent of those surveyed have at least one child in their class who has "no idea" how to use a book.

Channel 4 News, which broadcast the research last night, was told by one teacher: "Many of the children now go to sleep with a story from Alexa rather than a parent."

A survey found that families are relying on the virtual assistant to entertain their children—while some four and five-year-olds try to 'swipe' books as they are so addicted to mobile phones [File photo]

The following discussion the by piece by *Daily Mail* readers, shows an increasing anti-tech stance by this segment of the population. They want to go back to the good old days of manners, proper education of toddlers, traditional schooling like reading books, and more importantly, restoring the parental relationship and role by reading bedtime stories yourself to your child, not replacing parents with machines like a Virtual Assistant device, a robot, a Smart TV, a permanently online tablet, a smartphone or gaming terminal.

But as I searched for further media coverage of this Channel 4 breaking news story, I found disconcerting headlines repeating the findings. From 2013! And 2018! What does that mean? Even though the earlier breaking news stories, which were founded again on government-backed or state-run polling of primary school teachers and kindergarten carers, did not mention Amazon Alexa as it was prior to the market dominance of this branded device, they had the same findings.

Kids starting schools in nappies, unsocialized, unable to speak the English language in a rudimentary form or full sentences, low attention span, not being familiar with books, and very low on literacy and verbal skills. In fact, earlier reports and studies had already dubbed this phenomenon in Britain as the "Education Underclass." Then enter Amazon Alexa, which in its own marketing material online, touts that it can only enhance a young child's educational experience and support learning by reading to children.

Curiously apart from the *Daily Mail* take up of the Channel 4 2019 reportage, the only other reference I found quickly online was a discussion on the famous www.mumsnet.com I read through the comments section in the thread that began the discussion about the Channel 4 piece the night before. Quite unexpectedly, a number of mothers, in fact the majority of comments were trying to downplay the whole situation, one even saying it wasn't reliable data because "only 100 teachers were interviewed." Others justified late toilet training, dummy sucking, nappies in school and so on.

Relevant to the backlash against Amazon Alexa reading to children were the repeatedly defensive reactions of these British mothers on Mumsnet. They didn't actually name Amazon or Alexa but referred to the whole digitization phenomenon that everyone was actually digitized and reading most material online. From books to magazines. A typical comment was "I often catch myself trying to swipe magazine pages" or "I catch myself looking at the top of the page for the time, or tap a book page to turn it" [8] In other words, these mothers on Mumsnet were endorsing the encroachment of interactive tech in their daily lives, AI or otherwise. What was good enough for Mum as a willing Digital Native, was defensible for the toddlers' behavior in the first classroom of their young lives.

I wrote about the positive effects of 2D and 3D avatars disrupting advertising by being more transparent about users opting in and then the Return on Investment for advertisers with automated direct metrics on

---

[8] Reference, Mumsnet consulted on September 21, 2019. Screenshot not taken due to privacy regulations. However you can search on their site for this "thread" if you accept the Mumsnet cookies from their platform i.e. so you can read this public conversation without having to join as a member.

human–machine interaction and conversion rates, there belies a real danger of "ads by stealth." So without ethical opt ins of users either under the GDPR or elsewhere. Take a look at this CNET promotion (is meant to be an article but it reads like an advertorial). The tech journalist uncritically lists all of Amazon Alexa's "awesome" capabilities without once questioning how the obvious advertisers behind each skill is making money out of you innocently asking a listening device for a recipe, the weather or to turn on switches in your home.[9]

Food and drink

- If you're anything like me, you have no idea which wines pair well with which food. Fortunately, the *MySomm* skill will tell you. Just ask, "Alexa, ask Wine Gal what goes with a pot roast?"
- The same goes for beer and the *What beer?* skill. The invocation for this particular skill is clever, making the phrasing natural and easy to remember. Just say, "Alexa, ask what beer goes with ramen."
- To kick up your home-bartending skills a notch, enable *The Bartender*. You can ask what a drink is made of, and it will tell you the ingredients and the recipe. The answers are a lot to take in for a single response all at once, but this skill can definitely help you dissect your favorite cocktails.
- To double-check what internal temperature is considered safe when cooking different meats, use *Meat Thermometer*. Say, "Alexa, ask Meat Thermometer what is the best temperature for steak."
- For recipes and food recommendations, try the *Best Recipes* skill. You can find recipes based on up to three ingredients and narrow the results to breakfast, lunch, or dinner. To get started, say, "Alexa, tell Best Recipes I'm hungry" or "Alexa, ask Best Recipes what's for dinner."

---

[9] https://cnet.com/how-to/amazon-echo-most-useful-alexa-skills/

- Similarly, *Meal Idea* will give you recipe ideas that call for common, everyday items you likely already have in your pantry. It's suggested things like bone soup (out of canned tomato soup and elbow noodles) and a salad made of salad greens, canned beets and goat cheese. At least one of those sounds great.
- One of my personal favorite skills is *Domino's*. You can *place your Domino's Easy Order* just by speaking, "Alexa, open Dominc's and place my Easy Order." You can also track the status of an order you've placed by saying," Alexa, open Domino's to track my order."
- If *Pizza Hut* is your jam, there's a skill for that, too. To get started, first enable the skill, link your account and say, "Alexa, tell Pizza Hut to place an order."
- Starbucks lets you place an order using Alexa with the *Starbucks Reorder* skill. After you enable the skill, you will need to link your account. The skill will not work unless you've previously placed a mobile order with the Starbucks app on Android or iOS. It can place an order at one of the last 10 Starbucks locations you've visited in person. You can also check your account balance and switch between your five previous mobile orders.

Fitness

- For those familiar with the *7-Minute Workout*, you'll be happy to learn there is a skill for the famous workout available on Alexa speakers. Say, "Alexa, open 7-Minute Workout." The workout will begin. You can pause and resume workouts as needed.
- Similarly, there is a skill for a *5-Minute Plank Workout*. This skill walks you through five minutes of various planks with a 10-second break between each.
- If you wear a Fitbit tracker on your wrist, you can enable the *Fitbit* skill. With this skill, you can ask Alexa about your progress or how you slept the night before. Before you can use the skill, however, you will need to link your

> Fitbit account by going to the skill page at *alexa.amazon.
> com* and linking your accounts.
>
> - For tracking your food, you can use the *Track by Nutritio-
>   nix* skill, which lets you record your food intake using your
>   voice, or ask for caloric values of foods. (Alexa does the lat-
>   ter by default.) Say things like, "Alexa, tell Food Tracker to
>   log a cup of almond milk" or "Alexa, ask Food Tracker how
>   many calories are in two eggs and three slices of bacon."
> - Each day, *Guided Meditation* will give you a different
>   meditation routine, ranging from three to eight minutes. If
>   you're not digging the current routine, you can say, "Alexa,
>   play next" to skip to the next exercise.
>
> Read more: *The best Alexa commands for exercise, better sleep and
> stress relief.*

Anyone with any experience of interacting with media, whether it is
TV, print or digital, understands that the business model is frequently:
user watches ads = user buys advertised stuff + makes money for the ad
platform and the manufacturer or provider of said stuff. Clearly by simply
asking for everyday needs like what to cook, how to exercise, even how
to sleep, you are providing the "sponsor" or advertiser behind the freely
given Skill precious data about *you*, your daily habits, your preferences for
buying stuff, and most importantly, how much you are prepared to shell
out thus creating a track record of your spending.

This is gold in the new Data is Oil era. And we are unclear through
the advertorials and online incessant pitching of the dominant, essentially
monopoly power providing these "free" services into your car, home, and
very bedroom, how much we are actually paying for it in terms of privacy
and data protection.

Even viewing this slideshow of images of what Amazon Alexa can do
for me, embedded within the CNET article discussed earlier,[10] I am being
tracked by CNET, Amazon, and who knows which third party advertisers

---

[10] https://cnet.com/pictures/coolest-things-to-do-with-your-amazon-echo-alexa/17/

Figure 6.3 © *Realfiction, Copenhagen, 2019. Mixed Reality experiences will become ever more sophisticated and overpowering for the senses. Here a woman immerses herself in the hologram illusions of buildings and objects projected over her Real Time perception of a night cityscape. Is it art or a commercial experience? The convergence seems to be necessary in the early 21st century's new Experience Economy giving way to CX tech and innovations like the ones discussed in this book*

who want my cookies for marketing purposes. Once opted in, how can a user ever opt out?

To ensure that the future of our digital lives entails diversity and insight, right now there needs to be more freewheeling exchange and less cautious interaction only ever orchestrated and controlled environment university seminars, academic conferences and even the trade show panel debates that can end up being "safe spaces" for peer only meetings. If we fail to get this dialogue between theorists and practitioners firmly established sustainably, we risk what I call disconnectivity.

This occurs when the theorizing on the grand topics of the "ethics of Artificial Intelligence" and how to "control the risks" presented by some uses of AI bots and ubiquitous Virtual Assistants and Cognitive Interfaces actually become irrelevant because they are disconnected from the Mixed Reality of this exciting new world of human–machine interaction. The "Posthumanist Age," as I explained in the Dedication pages of this book. Enjoy enhanced connectivity and be mindful of who you are excluding and including in your exchanges about this ever riveting subject that

Figure 6.4 A large robot with finely-tuned movements cooks popcorn autonomously, i.e. unsupervised by humans on its own, in a kitchen despite what many would perceive to be a high risk, even dangerous situation and task—for robotics and AI. Taken from the film "Hi, AI" by Isa Willinger © Kloos & Co Medien, Berlin, 2019

will soon become an empowering aspect to our everyday lives, as soon as the hype dissipates and we begin to experience a multitude of (mixed) realities.

Figure 6.5 China is now a huge manufacturer of robots with AI interactivity such as reading emotions and recognizing faces of individuals. Meanwhile Japan is reported to be manufacturing several thousand new types of robot every month. Japanese robots are often humanoid like this one with "convincing skin" and realistic blinking eyes. However this has not yet completely removed them from the "Valley of the Uncanny" whereby human-looking and acting robots "freak out" ordinary people who feel uneasy that the robot is almost like them, but not quite. Taken from the film "Hi, AI" by Isa Willinger © Kloos & Co Medien, Berlin, 2019

Glossary

Dictionary of Tech Terms and Industry Jargon

Glossary 1 © Realfiction, Copenhagen, 2019. A holographic butterfly flutters in a burst of color for the entertainment of shoppers and passersby

AB Testing or the Last Stage of the Workflow

This is when the commissioning client is given the near finished chatbot to test in their own time, on a "hidden page." This website page is at a link or URL that the client can distribute to their team, management, communications and marketing people and any other stakeholders.

The almost complete chatbot will be live 24/7 for important feedback about how it is working on different devices, browsers and in various languages. It is the crucial time when the client gives feedback about whether their expectations have been met and if not, they explain where the chatbot needs to be improved.

Even if the client is happy with the performance of the bot, the bot developer should be seeking further input about the content and messaging of the Conversational AI. This is essential as the first iteration of the bespoke bot forms the foundation or framework for all other versions, later input and improvements.

Once the chatbot "draft" on the hidden URL or page has been improved to everyone's satisfaction, then the chatbot will be given a Release Date. When the 2D bot is for a website, then the client's webmaster needs to be involved. If its social media, then the manager of the feed for example, Facebook's Messenger platform needs to be in the loop.

For complex 3D AI bot holograms, we suggest a low key installation public facing release date, then after a few weeks or months of the bot getting to know its users and vice versa through live on boarding then hold a press conference or launch event with stakeholders and company guests.

Accelerator, see Incubator
Algorithm or Source Code, see Proprietary Algorithm
Artificial Intelligence or AI
This has sadly become a hackneyed term to the point where it either loses a lot of meaning or becomes confusing for those outside of the technology world. Even some scientists are confused by the jargon, so you shouldn't feel like there are strict rules for becoming an "insider" in the AI world!

AI is "sexy," it goes without saying. This has led to the main reason for writing this textbook: to dispel the hype and misleading definitions when it is used in conjunction to define or describe chatbots and bots "powered by AI."

It can mean the algorithms that crunch data, and analyze their own mistakes—see the definition in this Glossary of Machine Learning and Deep Learning. Robots are also said to have AI if they can correct their actions or "thoughts" so for example the football playing tiny robots that pick themselves up when they fall and slowly use strategies they have learnt from past games.

Go the Chinese chess game that Deep Mind Technologies won in London before they were acquired by the U.S. tech giant Google and IBM

Watson's famous win at the TV quiz Jeopardy are the most famous examples. However, it is fairly narrow though deep AI applications, more like the Deep Learning described in this glossary under Machine Learning.

The Holy Grail is then General AI which would mean a humanoid robot capable of moving like us and more importantly making decisions like humans with a combination of reason, rationality, Emotional Intelligence, moral understanding and logic. And a dash of intuition which would be part of its EI equipment.

In terms of chatbots, it signals those AI bots that can also self-correct and learn from mistakes, minimal though they may be. In that way it as organic bot brain that can improve slowly but surely to provide a better CX or Customer Experience.

In my company's experience at the frontier of this Mixed Reality integration with voice, it can also mean the AI teaches the avatar how to recognize speech in accents and meaning, in any language. It learns through experiencing conversation. See also NLU and NLP in this glossary.

Augmented Reality, AR, see Mixed Reality
Automation, Automated Processes
In the corporate world, people talk a lot about automation. It began with heavy industry for example, Big robots manufacturing car parts, even whole cars, robotic arms replacing humans on assembly lines, robots in warehouses lifting boxes and now even searching for and delivering items to the humans facing the customers or B2B partners.

Automation for corporations usually means digitized processes that make the work flow more streamlined. Yes, it also means job losses for humans unless HR can redeploy them in another part of the company. An example of AI automating things can be an algorithm writing a text for a journalist or working for doctors using image recognition to screen xrays and diagnostic results for example, trying to spot cancer signs or eye deterioration.

Avatar
This means the figure like a cartoon or image of a person that represents the bot brain. Avatar choice has been used for ages in computer gaming and signifies the player choosing a face or image that symbolizes them during the game. It is like the ID for your profile instead of an actual photo.

In botification it means the independent entity that is the interactive character or figure that is the "machine" in the human-machine interation we have been discussing in this book. As a cognitive interface, you could create a bot brain without an avatar. But then my company has found in pilots and beta testing that people just using voice for example, speaking at your smartphone to a Virtual Assistant without an avatar character to focus on, relate to or anthromorphise, is a deterrent to widespread use. Humans like to anthromorphise the avatar, robot or hologram, humanoid or animal like, object or symbol.

BaaS, Bots as a Service

Taken from Software as a Service or SaaS, Bots as a Service or the abbreviation BaaS indicates the general industry that operates in the cloud. That means chatbots and 3D bots can be run and hosted remotely, without having to be installed on the client's servers or hardware systems.

My company has called itself AI BaaS in order to buck the trend of New Tech startups with really weird names. AI BaaS basically says what we do—Bots as a Service with Artificial Intelligence. However we were guilty of nerdy venture names with our former one, velmai Ltd. Virtual Empirical Lifeforms with Multimedia AI. I rest my case for purchasers not having to second guess cryptic company acronyms!

Botification, to botify

It is a new term that can be applied when a surface or machine becomes cognitive. Easy examples are when you can talk or interact with your vacuum cleaner, fridge, TV and car! So not just a Home Environment also self-driving and hybrid or semiautomated vehicles.

Essentially, it means that you put an avatar into the human-machine interaction. For example, if you are interacting with a survey say on SurveyMonkey or an online form, then that is human-machine interaction in its simplest form. When you bot a chatbot into that communication, so a bot like our Sophia the Market Researcher (see the following screenshot image from the video demo) runs the survey, you can say that the online questionnaire has been botified.

When a car has a personality in terms of voice, so not necessarily a visual avatar, then that vehicle has been botified. Same goes for an Apple phone—Siri performs the botification. We are still exploring ways to botify everything from your personal appliances to your wearables. See also "Cognitive Interfaces."

Bots, see Intelligent Virtual Assistants
Chatbots, or Bots, see Intelligent Virtual Assistants
Cognitive Interface, CI or Cognitive Market, Conversational AI, Conversational Commerce
As discussed earlier in the definitions of Avatar and Artificial Intelligence in this glossary, it denotes human-machine interaction. Essentially the conversation between the computer and the human must show evidence that

(a) the entity or avatar is responding spontaneously if not creatively
(b) it demonstrates that it can learn over time if corrected repeatedly
(c) that it can build its knowledge base and Emotional Intelligence through increased interaction with humans

Customer Experience or CX, developed from UX or User Experience
This is essential for customer satisfaction. If the user has not had a good experience with the technology, they will not re-engage with it. It therefore loses its commercial value if the tech's poor CX leads to low user numbers and bad quality interactions. It will not create the desired ROI or Return on Investment.

Deep Learning, see Machine Learning
Early Adopters, see First Movers
Emerging Tech, see New Technologies
Greenfield Project, see Pilot
Human-Machine Interaction, see Intelligent Virtual Assistants and/ or see Artificial Intelligence
Immersive Reality, see Mixed Reality
Industrie 4.0
This term originated in Germany in the early 2000s. It denotes the 4th Industrial Revolution and is a concept referred to outside of Germany as the next industrial revolution, post industrial and the Digital Age or Age of Convergence.

A lot of German government policies about growth and economic planning were focused on Industrie 4.0 which has also come to be known as Digitalisierung or digitization (see the definition in this glossary).

Even in 2019 there is a widespread fear that German businesses, especially SMEs, are not using digital technologies optimally, whether it is the cloud and Software as a Service or simply marketing adequately online with social media and integrated marketing campaigns that leverage the web.

Industrie 5.0 is thus focused on Digitalisierung, Artificial Intelligence and moving toward Quantum computing which is one of Germany's strengths in Informatik or Information Technology.

Intelligent Virtual Assistants, IVAs. Also known as chatbots and bots, Virtual Assistants

Intelligent Virtual Assistants as many Americans in the field like to term them, are the Next Gen chatbots. They have moved on from manually coded chatbots that relied on fairly basic Natural Language Processing, as was the case from the 1950s to the early 2000s.

Then we began to see the beginnings of Conversational AI and cleverer bots with improved Natural Language Understanding. The smarter Virtual Assistants or chatbots were part of the bot Hype Cycle as defined by the analyst firm Gartner, where after Mark Zuckerberg announcing notification was the future as did Microsoft's Satya Nadella, the investment boom and Use Cases flourished. This financial rush really only happened in the Silicon Valley and less so in Europe.

The defining element distinguishing a standard basic chatbot and AI bots is Emotional Intelligence (EI). Or a more complex form of communicating as I describe in my *VentureBeat* article from 2016 "Why Chatbots are so disruptive."[1] EI applied to advanced chatbots means that they can not only imitate humans to convince users they are not talking to a machine, they can also surprise them by showing intuition or emotional qualities like kindness and empathy.

In this higher level or better performing stage of AI bots, the human machine interaction provides a satisfying experience. The user may realize

---

[1] VB .

that they are talking with a machine but they have moments that they think the bot could be almost human like or humanoid. The classic Turing Test goal for all bot developers!

Iterations

This means the latest version of the bot in development. It can also mean a clone or new interpretation of a bot brain. So based on the foundation character or personality of the avatar, the developers then release a similar bot but with newer content or quite different character. However, some of the original content is still the basis of the chatbot.

Machine Learning, also Deep Learning and Neural Networks

Has now replaced Neural Networks as the term of choice that signifies source code that is able to learn from its mistakes and gradually improve its knowledge base on its own. Abbreviated in tech circles as ML, it is forming the foundation of much of data mining these days which is also called Deep Learning when the algorithm is able to self-correct.

Machine Learning is being applied to biotech for better diagnoses of medical conditions, as well as green tech for crunching numbers and providing advice. Similarly, fintech has long used Deep Learning and the legacy codes are now being rejuvenated or replaced with AI which means in this instance Machine Learning.

Mixed Reality, Mixed Reality Installations or Experiences, also Immersive Reality, including Augmented Reality (AR) and Virtual Reality (VR)

This is a term referring to a mixture of media forms such as holograms, robots, Virtual Reality and Augmented Reality. It is a catch all term that also indicates usually speech recognition in the MR mix, so the hybrid tech is voice based. My company is now specializing in bespoke holograms with multimedia elements that can include VR experiences. We can also integrate our chatbot algorithm into some Augmented Reality algorithms that allow integration. That then becomes the Mixed Reality experience which will be key for the upcoming Experience Economy.

Virtual Reality is generally defined as people wearing special glasses that give them the 3D experience that is very intense spatially and in most sensory ways even including smell with some applications. Very few applications work without the eyewear to alter human's perceptions of what they are seeing.

Critics have pointed to the induced nausea of these experiences while fans say VR can even have healing powers to cure affected users of PTSD and phobias by showing them the feared images and making them relive the traumatic or feared experience. VR is widely used commercially to promote travel and tourism deals and of course in gaming or computer games.

Augmented Reality is the opposite and rarely requires special glasses or eyewear to make the AR experience work. It most commonly works by the user holding up a tablet or smartphone over a surface which then "pops up" as a 3D video or film of what the experience has been designed for.

AR apps have most frequently used by the travel and tourism sector to promote sightseeing spectacles or car manufactures that show the latest model with the chosen color, tires or features in the extended 3D virtual image.

Natural Language Processing (NLP) or Natural Language Understanding (NLU)

This is a type of basic programming of the more simplistic chatbots, nearly all 2D avatars operating online. The early ones were live on websites only. Then with the advent of Instant Messaging platforms, a new breed of NLP chatbots were developed for those mediums. So the avatars were able to IM or chat with users via the apps that allowed botification, that is, chatbot integration.

NLU claims to be a more complex rendering of the legacy NLP language processing to enable these 2D chatbots to demonstrate more comprehension and sentiment. They are not however to be classified as Cognitive Interfaces nor Conversational AI. They can be categorized as successful legacy examples of Conversational Commerce before the rise of Mixed Reality installations with botified interfaces like 3D AI holograms.

Speech Recognition, ASR or Voice tech, see Voice
Three dimensional interfaces, 3D AI bots

This is the cutting edge. So far only my company is doing it for 3D holograms that interact. There are many pilots at trade shows, most of them are recordings and you can converse with them. There have been a few interactive attempts but none have made it to market. Deutsche Bahn for robot heads as Wayfinder and timetable info. Pepper robots and other robots in Japan, South Korea and China for retail deployments.

See also "Cognitive Interfaces" for 3D bots.

Two dimensional bots, 2D bots or Instant Messaging interfaces, see Intelligent Virtual Assistants (IVAs)
UX, User Experience, see CX Customer Experience
Virtual Assistants, see IVAs or Intelligent Virtual Assistants
Virtual Reality, see Mixed Reality
Voice, voice-based, also Speech Recognition (ASR)
We are now seeing chatbot conferences replaced by voice tech summits. This means that more bot developers are seeing the advantages of literally "plugging in" a voice to give their avatar more personality, much like making it animated instead of just two dimensional and static. Not all voice bots are the same though. You may interact with a basic NLP chatbot that has been given voice. This means it is using speech recognition software to understand what you are saying to it, then "parsing" the reply back to you as speech instead of its usual text messages.

For 3D avatars, voice is optimal because it fits with the overall Mixed Reality industrial design. They recognize speech and also dialects with the better ASR plug ins. This niche is developing rapidly as a core competence.

The voice tech people will enable more bot developers to plug in to their specialist audio software which is an advanced form of Natural Language Processing but not necessarily standalone Artificial Intelligence. It needs to be combined with a good "bot brain" that has demonstrated cognitive thinking in order to be classified as Conversational AI or a Cognitive Interface.

Voice activated, see Wake Words
Wake Words
The most famous voice-based bot using wake words is of course Amazon Alexa. The wake words are "Alexa" in this instance, which is said to awaken the machine to respond. It has been shown that Amazon's devices including Echo and Dot are "always listening to you" potentially, after a number of exposes by the media, such as Der Spiegel.

The reportage proved that the devices had recorded their owners in the most intimate and private moments without permission, that is, they had not been given the wake words to signal them to listen. The devices did not respond either to alert the users that were active. Instead Amazon HQ illegally recorded people's private conversations and sent them to back offices around the world to be "transcribed and analysed so that our software and speech recognition could be improved." See the Voice definition for what speech recognition is.

Wake words can be used by 2D chatbots as well as 3D bots. For instance, Samsung wants you to say "Bixby" to awaken its built in chatbot, as of course the most famous smartphone Virtual Assistant of all, Siri on Apple devices. Microsoft has put 2D bot Cortana onto its PCs and desktops in the hope that users will speak to her and use the wake words to activate this Virtual Assistant built into every Microsoft device. Many bot developers are following suit, especially voice-based IVAs. My company AI BaaS also uses this feature.

Glossary2 © Realfiction, Copenhagen, 2019. The next generation watch fascinated as a hologram rocket takes off in full sound and color in Mixed Reality. This means the rocket is projected onto the real ocean that you see behind the MR device or "Deep Frame," as the manufacturer Realfiction calls their product, creating the experience in Real Time, even though the holographic performance was created in a studio or lab to be deployed using real life settings and audio

About the Author

The technologist **Tania Peitzker** is the CEO and co-owner of AI Bots as a Service. This Mixed Reality German venture builds "bot brains" or AI bot holograms for multilingual 2D and 3D bespoke avatars. The unique humanoid or unisex characters feature voice or speech recognition (ASR) and speak over 130 languages on any device.

AI BaaS has invested over a decade of R&D in its own proprietary algorithm for customizable botification; it's called VAIP [Virtual Artificially Intelligent Patois]. To get the very latest summary of her life and work, you can listen to a 2019 radio interview in her original hometown of Cairns with the ABC (Australian Broadcasting Corporation). It's 10 minutes and online as a podcast on her portfolio site www.taniapeitzker.expert

An Australian-German with a doctorate in *Anglistik* from the University of Potsdam, she's now an Adjunct Professor for AI Management and digitization at various business schools in Europe. Due to Britain's years of "Brexit upheavals," she commutes to her German technology venture's headquarters in Munich—in Bavaria where her father hails from—from Britain and spends much of her time on the European Continent.

© *Tania Peitzker, Selfie on the shores of Saint Jean Cap Ferrat, 2018*

bots as a service

© *Company logo of AI BaaS UG in Munich, 2019*

Index

OTHER TITLES IN THE HUMAN RESOURCE MANAGEMENT AND ORGANIZATIONAL BEHAVIOR COLLECTION

- *Our Glassrooms* by Dhruva Trivedy
- *Creating the Accountability Culture* by Yvonnne Thompson
- *Conflict and Leadership* by Christian Muntean
- *Power Quotes* by Danai Krokou
- *Negotiating with Winning Words* by Michael Schatzki
- *21st Century Skills for Non-Profit Managers* by Don Macdonald and Charles Oham

Announcing the Business Expert Press Digital Library

Concise e-books business students need for classroom and research

This book can also be purchased in an e-book collection by your library as

- a one-time purchase,
- that is owned forever,
- allows for simultaneous readers,
- has no restrictions on printing, and
- can be downloaded as PDFs from within the library community.

Our digital library collections are a great solution to beat the rising cost of textbooks. E-books can be loaded into their course management systems or onto students' e-book readers.
The **Business Expert Press** digital libraries are very affordable, with no obligation to buy in future years. For more information, please visit **www.businessexpertpress.com/librarians**. To set up a trial in the United States, please email **sales@businessexpertpress.com**.

www.ingramcontent.com/pod-product-compliance
Lightning Source LLC
Chambersburg PA
CBHW061317220326
41599CB00026B/4913